BARNET

Supporting
Speaking and
Listening

0

2011

More titles in the *Helping Hands* series:

Supporting Spelling by Sylvia Edwards, ISBN 1-84312-208-1

Supporting Reading by Angela Wilson and Julie Scanlon, ISBN 1-84312-210-3

Supporting Writing by Sylvia Edwards, ISBN 1-84312-209-X

A selection of other books for teaching assistants:

A Handbook for Learning Support Assistants: Teachers and Assistants Working Together by Glenys Fox, ISBN 1-84312-081-X

Assisting Learning and Supporting Teaching: A Practical Guide for the Teaching Assistant in the Classroom by Anne Watkinson, ISBN 1-85346-794-4

Supporting Children with Behaviour Difficulties: A Guide for Assistants in Schools by Glenys Fox, ISBN 1-85346-764-2

The Essential Guide for Competent Teaching Assistants: Meeting the National Occupational Standards at Level 2 by Anne Watkinson, ISBN 1-84312-008-9

The Essential Guide for Experienced Teaching Assistants: Meeting the National Occupational Standards at Level 2 by Anne Watkinson, ISBN 1-84312-009-7

Successful Study: Skills for Teaching Assistants by Christine Ritchie and Paul Thomas, ISBN 1-84312-106-9

Understanding Children's Learning: A Text for Teaching Assistants edited by Claire Alfrey, ISBN 1-84312-069-0

Supporting Speaking and Listening

Angela Wilson

Series edited by Sylvia Edwards and Angela Wilson

 **David Fulton** Publishers

David Fulton Publishers Ltd
The Chiswick Centre, 414 Chiswick High Road, London W4 5TF

www.fultonpublishers.co.uk

First published in Great Britain in 2004 by David Fulton Publishers

10 9 8 7 6 5 4 3 2 1

Note: The right of Angela Wilson to be identified as the author of this work has been asserted by her in accordance with the Copyright, Designs and Patents Act 1988.

Copyright © Angela Wilson 2004

British Library Cataloguing in Publication Data
A catalogue record for this book is available from the British Library.

David Fulton Publishers is a division of Granada Learning, part of ITV plc.

ISBN 1 84312 211 1

Typeset by FiSH Books
Printed and bound in Great Britain By Ashford Colour Press

Contents

In memory of Margery Graham

Acknowledgements

I am very grateful to all the students, colleagues and friends (and their children) who have contributed in various ways to the production of this book. In particular, I would like to thank Emma Constantine and Reuben, Hilda Johnson, Zoe Tribe (and Amy and Ethan) and Joan Zorn. Above all I would like to thank my husband for being so unfailingly patient and long-suffering.

Overview

The aim of this book is to offer some practical suggestions, thoughts and ideas on:

- *The importance of speaking and listening in everyday life.* What are our goals for children in this area of human experience? How can parents, teachers and other adults support children in the achievement of these goals?

- *How we all manage the business of talking to each other.* Are there different kinds of talk? What makes one variety different from another? How do we know when to talk and what kinds of talk to use?

- *Learning to talk.* How do babies and young children (0–4) get started on these most complicated systems we call 'language'? What happens when they leave their homes and have to talk to people who don't know them so well?

- *Whether speaking, as well as listening, helps children to learn.* What does it mean to learn by speaking? What kinds of activities would we need to provide for this to happen? What kinds of classroom organisation and structure?

- *How we can tell if children are making progress in speaking and listening.* A look at the different kinds of records we might keep. Some thoughts on assessment strategies but also a reminder of the importance of spontaneous, unplanned opportunities for assessment.

Who is the book for?

The book is part of a series intended mainly for people who are already, or who intend to become, teaching assistants in primary schools. It covers a range of general issues concerned with speaking and listening in the mainstream curriculum although it is hoped that it will also be useful for those working specifically to support special needs children and children for whom English is an additional language.

Introduction

Were you surprised to find speaking and listening featuring alongside reading and writing in a series such as this? If your own education took place before 1960, you will probably remember your English lessons in primary school as concerned almost exclusively with learning to read and with aspects of writing including grammar, spelling and punctuation. Talking in class was probably frowned upon, especially of course when the teacher was talking. And teachers talked for a lot of the time. In the playground, however, everyone talked a lot: they certainly didn't seem to need any lessons in how to do it. So where has this idea of incorporating talk into the curriculum come from, and what exactly does it involve? These are issues which will be taken up in more detail in the chapters of this book. Here I want to make some general points so that you can see more clearly the kinds of topics covered.

Learning how, learning through and learning about talk

As this heading suggests there are three aspects to considering talk and I shall touch on each of them briefly here. You can find out more in the rest of this book and as you read on you will find suggestions of a few other books, articles and documents listed at the end of each chapter if you want to read more widely.

Learning how to talk

Perhaps we tend to see this process as complete, for most children, by the age of four or so. It's true that they have learned an impressive amount by then – Chapter 3 looks in more detail at what they have learned. However, living in today's world raises many more complex issues than a four-year-old will meet. To deal with them, we need to go on building our talk skills all through our lives. In Chapter 1, I will ask you to think about the wide range of reasons for talking that life throws up at us in the twenty-first century, and in Chapter 2 I will review the ways in which we need to extend children's language abilities to cope with these demands.

Learning through talk

How people learn is a huge topic and a crucial one for anyone concerned with schools. Many children are told when they are about to start school that they must 'Sit quietly and listen to the teacher.' Teachers are sometimes, or were until about 40 years ago, seen as founts of knowledge and children the 'empty vessels' or the 'blank pages' for the teacher to work on. In the sixties, for a variety of reasons, people began to question whether in fact teachers talked too much and children not enough. Perhaps learning was not exclusively a passive activity, something we had 'done to us', but something that had to be engaged with actively. An invention as ordinary (for us) as a portable tape recorder, left running discreetly in the classroom, made it possible for researchers to become aware of the impressive amount of learning that went on when children were allowed to talk among themselves. This view of children as capable of learning from each other was given official approval in 1975 by a government-sanctioned document, *The Bullock Report*. Learning through talk, however, has had a chequered history in schools since then. It is now very much back on the official agenda and I will look at what can be done to support this mode of learning, and how, in Chapters 4, 5 and 6.

Learning about talk

One of the most controversial areas as far as language teaching is concerned these days is how much children should be taught explicitly about their language. We all have a great deal of implicit knowledge: on the whole, most of us can talk, read and write well enough to cope with our lives, though we may struggle a bit on some occasions. But we might be concerned if we had to describe what we had just said or written:

I've just uttered a complex sentence with a subordinating conjunction and two verbs in the past perfect tense.

It sounds impossible – but we do it all the time without actually being aware. Does this matter? Does it matter if we don't know a noun from a verb or an adjective? The government thinks it does, and has introduced a great deal of knowledge about language into the curriculum, especially through the National Literacy Strategy.

Teaching knowledge about language in a context

If you are one of those people I referred to earlier who was educated in the forties or fifties, you may remember having to work on grammar. Unfortunately, much of this work was separated from other activities such as reading and writing, which led many people to think that grammar was irrelevant to their needs. Those educated in the sixties and after probably know little, if anything, about it, unless they have studied the grammar of a foreign language. Nowadays, what is often called 'knowledge about language' is back on the agenda, but ideally it is being tackled in a different way. Whenever we write or talk, we are making a selection from the grammar and vocabulary of the language to enable us to put our meanings across in the most suitable way for our purpose and our audience or reader. To have a wide selection of language to choose from is immensely empowering for children. I hope that everything you take from this book will enable you to enthuse children to become confident language users themselves, and help them to be sensitive to and critical of the language used by others.

Speech/writing similarities and contrasts

Very often, speaking has to be done 'on the hoof' – we don't have much time to choose our words. This is one of the principal differences between speaking and writing and I shall have more to say about this in Chapter 2. For now I just want to say that I believe passionately that learning *about* language – and this applies to language in all its manifestations, by word of mouth, on a screen, on paper – is not something that children find boring or off-putting. Provided it is done properly, it is just as interesting as learning *about* the Tudors or *about* fractions – in fact, more interesting because it permeates every aspect of our lives.

How can we tell if we've been successful?

Nowadays, as you are sure to have noticed if you've already started working in a school, there is a requirement to be much more accountable for what we do. Teachers are required to set targets and to provide evidence of the extent to which they have been achieved. One of the reasons why speaking and listening, after 40 years, could still be considered the Cinderella of the language curriculum is probably because there has never been a national achievement test in this area. Assessment of any kind is tricky – are we measuring according to some absolute standard or are we looking at the progress each child has made since starting school? Some children may have had little or no experience of speaking English in their homes. Are we sure exactly what it is we are testing? Is reading, for example, a question of 'saying written words aloud' or is there more to it than that? (For more on this particular issue see *Supporting Reading* in this series.) Is talking something to do with 'speaking nicely and clearly'? I hope I've already begun to convince you that it's much more than that. And how do we pin talk down so that we can assess it? It's much more difficult than taking home a pile of tests to mark. I shall look at these issues in more detail in Chapter 7.

Chapter 1

How does talk fit into our everyday lives?

The range of contexts for talk

To help you to understand more about why talk is considered important in the curriculum of a primary school, I would like you to start by thinking about yourself as a speaker and listener. To see how this activity has relevance for your work in school, see the quotations at the end of this chapter. If a market researcher stopped you in the street and asked if you would consider yourself a good speaker what would you say? Perhaps, by switching to the term 'speaking' instead of 'talking' I have already made you think of giving speeches, opening fetes or even preaching a sermon. If you do not believe you are a good speaker (or even a good talker) why is that? What do you think lets you down? Would you like to be better at it? What would that involve?

Before you are tempted to run yourself down too much, take ten minutes to jot down all the purposes for talk you can recall being involved in over the course of a week or so. Be specific, e.g. don't just write 'persuading' but 'persuading partner to book a skiing holiday'. Include anything that was accomplished orally, even if very trivial, and telephone conversations. Also note down who you were speaking to (including yourself) and where you were at the time – in your kitchen, perhaps, or the school staff room. You could organise your notes in columns to look like this:

Purpose   Audience   Setting

I'm sure that long before ten minutes were up, you had a pretty long list. In today's world we increasingly accomplish aspects of our daily lives by talking rather than writing. And if we include texting by mobile phone, which is a sort of cross between speaking and writing, the list would be even longer.

If you look at your list again, you'll probably be able to highlight the examples of talk that come most easily to you as well as those that give you more problems – perhaps you even dread them. If you do not have any of these difficult situations on your list at present, think back to any occasions you found really challenging, however long ago.

What was on your list?

Purpose: the tasks we accomplish through talking

The first heading I asked you to consider was 'Purpose'. Which of the speaking situations comes so easily that the words just tumble out? Which do you find a challenge? Everyone's list will be different, of course, but I would suspect that the everyday gossip and dealing with daily life come into the 'easy' category for most people – although I must confess to finding conversations at the hairdresser's a bit of a challenge! Everyone else in the salon seems to participate in an endless series of glamorous holidays in far-flung places while my modest week in South Wales gives rise to no conversation at all. On a more serious note, it's very difficult sometimes to know what to say to a friend who has just lost a member of her family. The feelings are all there, but it's so difficult to put them into words without sounding banal.

Other purposes for talk that might have featured on your list could include chairing a meeting, summarising a discussion or persuading someone who was reluctant to take on a task. Each one calls for slightly different 'talk skills'.

Audience: who's taking part?

'Audience' is a slightly misleading word as I don't mean to imply someone who is listening and not saying anything. They may be, but it's more likely that they are joining in. However, it's a label I've got used to using so I hope you'll bear with me.

Look back at your list again. I asked you to rank the items on an 'easiest to most difficult' scale. So far, we've only discussed the nature of the task itself, but it's likely that the people involved will have a bearing on how you feel about the situation. Again, I can only speak from my own experience.

Numbers

I find that I can talk quite freely and informally in groups of up to eight or ten people. Twenty in the group implies, in my job, a class of some sort, and almost certainly requires me to do some prior planning and some organisation. Two hundred in the audience, as far as I'm concerned, implies quite a bit of stress and a degree of preparation such that I may well be reading my text aloud from prepared notes. I am extremely unlikely to be the person who calls out a question from the back of the crowded town hall. So the numbers of people involved is certainly a crucial factor for me.

Status

It's possible, of course, that even if there's only one person listening, if that person is an Ofsted inspector or someone who's about to interview you for a job you desperately want, you will still feel some degree of stress. You may take up a new hobby and join a group, all of whose members seem much more knowledgeable than you and use jargon you can scarcely understand. You may find yourself in a job with someone who has been in the post for years and seems incredibly experienced, emphasising how 'new' you feel. You can perhaps identify other examples from your own list where it was not the numbers of people involved but their status that was intimidating.

Setting

My last suggested heading asked you to think about where the talk took place. Even the head teacher interviewing you for a job will seem less intimidating if you are chatting over a cup of tea than if she is sitting behind her desk and you are facing her with the sun in your eyes. Classrooms on the first Monday back after the holidays can reduce people to silence because they have a chilly, unlived-in air. Windy days often seem to encourage children to scream and shout in the playground (and some-times in the classroom too). Some people can chat for hours on the telephone while others hate the lack of eye contact and find it hard to make their meanings clear without using gestures.

Of course, you may be impervious to aspects of the setting. You may be thinking so hard that you don't notice how cold it is. Or, in the interview situation, you may suddenly become horribly aware that there are governors sitting all round you, wondering what you will say next. It's how you feel about the task, the audience and the setting that matters – whether you find them supportive, stimulating, challenging, terrifying or whatever. You might find it interesting to compare your own responses to this activity with someone else's.

Speech as public performance

There's another aspect of speaking and listening which I feel I must emphasise: to some extent, it is always a performance and we run the risk, perhaps, of being laughed at if we get it wrong. Suppose you just dry up or something comes out the wrong way round, or in a squeaky voice – it doesn't matter too much in the privacy of your own kitchen (although the family may not let you forget it for weeks afterwards). But in a public place it could feel very humiliating. Also, once words are said, there's no taking them back – even if we apologise profusely for something we regret saying, nothing can take the impact of the words away entirely.

Another aspect of this 'performance' topic that can't be ignored is accent and dialect (for a fuller discussion of what these terms mean, see Chapter 2). Sadly, there are still a lot of people, even today, who feel ashamed of the way they make the sounds of English. They realise that they have a regional accent, that they don't sound 'posh' or 'plummy'. It's possible that some speakers feel uneasy about whether or not they are using the grammar of standard English. Should it be 'One of them books' or 'One of those books'? There are many people, of course, who are proud of their regional accents or who feel that accent and dialect don't matter a jot, especially in their own neighbourhood with their friends. To speak any other way might attract accusations of being 'toffee-nosed' or worse. Nevertheless, many of us feel some pressure, on occasions, to dress up our speech a bit, and this might cause feelings of strain or unease.

What can we learn from this activity which will help us in supporting children?

By now I hope you have a picture of yourself as an accomplished talker albeit perhaps with some areas of experience that cause you problems. As I have admitted myself, although I earn my living by talking with and to roomfuls of people, some occasions still render me tongue-tied. I have only been able to sketch in some examples of talking that can be challenging. Below, I will try to summarise a little more broadly from those examples.

Talking can be a problem for all of us when:

- The topic is one we have no personal experience of.
- The topic is not one we can work up any enthusiasm for – we find it boring or tedious. (Equally, being overwhelmed by emotion can render us tongue-tied.)
- Something about the people we are talking with intimidates us.
- The setting makes us feel uncomfortable in some way.
- We fear rejection, ridicule, 'put-down'.
- We find it impossible to find words that don't sound tired and banal from overuse.
- We can't get our ideas into the right order – we continually stop in mid-sentence and try to start again.
- We can't handle the jargon of the topic under discussion.
- We feel under pressure to say something and it 'comes out all wrong', perhaps unintentionally causing pain.
- We are ashamed of our accents (the way we make the sounds of English).
- We are ashamed of our dialects (we feel that our grammar and/or vocabulary is not standard English).

I hope the above list of 'difficulties' doesn't seem too daunting. My purpose in listing them is to make the point that even as adults, with experience of many years of living, working, building social relationships and so on, we can still struggle with some aspects of speaking and listening. Some of the aspects we find challenging are linked with the nature of the task – putting a lot of ideas into words in the right order perhaps, or summing up a complex series of events. Just as important are the social aspects – handling the relationships involved, particularly if we have to say something challenging or difficult for our listeners. This might involve choosing just the right word or adopting a certain emphasis or a conciliatory tone.

Children and talking

Most adults have had a fairly wide experience of talking for a variety of purposes and in a broad range of social situations. But what is the situation like for children who have had a much more limited range of experience of all kinds? An important point to remember here too is that children – both at home and at school – are almost continually subject to adult expectations. What do adults today expect as regards children's talking and listening?

Talk in the home

In December 2003, the government published some guidelines for schools on developing speaking and listening in Key Stages 1 and 2 (you will find quotes from these materials at the end of Chapters 1 and 2 and throughout this book). A journalist in *The Times*, commenting on the guidelines, pointed out how different adults' expectations seem to be now from, say, 40 or 50 years ago. Her own father, she recalled, if she dared to raise her voice at the meal table would thunder 'Efface yourself!' Children were to be seen and not heard.

Perhaps you are a parent or a grandparent. What do you like to see – or rather, hear – from a well brought-up child? If you are a grandparent, do you notice differences in conversations with children now from when your own children were young? I'm thinking here about what can be talked about, when and with whom, rather than issues to do with 'sloppy speech' – although you may have views on that too. (For a further discussion on encouraging children to 'speak nicely' see the next chapter.) Can you remember the last discussion you had with a child in your family? Would it have been about a film or a television programme you had seen together, or a book you had shared? Perhaps you planned an outing to go on together or looked forward to the visit of a friend or relative. On the other hand, given the busy lives we all lead, you may not have time for much discussion – or not much more than what to have for tea.

Gender issues

Do you make any distinctions between the boys and the girls in the family as regards speaking and listening? Do you ever hear adults saying something like 'Suzy is such a nice quiet girl' or 'Tom's so noisy all the time, but then, boys will be boys.' A government document claims that the 'characteristics of the talk of boys and girls often differ' (DfES/QCA 2003a: 12).

With young children, the real crunch may come over something they want but you feel they can't or shouldn't have. All this discussion and listening to their point of view is all very well, but there comes a moment when you insist that WHAT I SAY GOES AND THAT'S THE END OF IT!!

Parents will all have different views about the significance of talk in bringing up children. Attitudes change over time within one culture and there will be marked differences between cultures. Some children have been brought up to show great respect for their elders, never disagreeing with them or answering back – perhaps not even looking them directly in the eye. It's a good idea to make yourself familiar with the range not only of home languages but also of cultural expectations in any class or group you are working with. Some children may be experiencing particularly difficult culture clashes and this may be an aspect of school life that you can help them with. There is no doubt that in the primary schools of today, all children will be expected, as far as possible, to become confident, articulate speakers.

In subsequent chapters in the book I will explore the journeys the child must take towards becoming a fully fledged 'talker', but in the next chapter I want to look more closely at some of the choices we make, and should help children to make, from the vast store of the English language, in order to put our thoughts, ideas and feelings into words.

Summary

In this chapter I have looked at:

- A range of contexts for talk that occurs frequently in today's world.
- Three aspects of what I mean by talk contexts:
  - purpose
  - audience
  - setting
- Adults' expectations of children as talkers.

Further reading

DfEE/QCA (1999) *The National Curriculum: Handbook for Primary Teachers in England*. London: DfEE/QCA.

DfEE/QCA (2000) *Curriculum Guidance for the Foundation Stage*. London: DfEE/QCA.

DfES/QCA (2003a) *Speaking, Listening and Learning: Working with Children in Key Stages 1 and 2. Handbook*. London: DfES/QCA.

DfES/QCA (2003b) *Speaking, Listening and Learning: Working with Children in Key Stages 1 and 2. Teaching Objectives and Classroom Activities*. London: DfES/QCA.

Curriculum Guidance for the Foundation Stage **(DfEE/QCA 2000)**
A major role in teaching involves extending children's language sensitively while acknowledging and showing respect for home languages, local dialects and any forms of augmentative communication that children may be using. (p. 23)

National Curriculum: Programme of Study for Speaking and Listening **(DfEE/QCA 1999)**

Key Stage 1 (pp. 44–5)
Pupils should be taught how speech varies:
a) in different circumstances
b) to take account of different listeners

Key Stage 2 (pp. 50–2)

Pupils should be taught how language varies:

a) according to context and purpose

b) between standard and dialect forms

c) between spoken and written forms

Speaking, Listening and Learning: Working with Children in Key Stages 1 and 2 (DfES/QCA 2003a)

The curriculum for speaking and listening must . . . give due weight to the distinctiveness of talk. (p. 7)

In the whole range of interactive situations from, for example, informal conversation to formal interview, meaning is mainly constructed collaboratively. (p. 7)

Actual talk varies far more (than talk that is written down in books) and children need to be taught how, when and why such variety happens and how to use this repertoire effectively. There are particular challenges for children learning English as an additional language to capture the meaning of idioms and different language varieties, including spoken standard English. (p. 8)

Social relationships are mostly enacted through talk. Levels of intimacy or formality may be tried out and instant feedback means constant adjustment of tone, register or content . . . Acceptability of talk in different contexts, as indicated by its reception, is vital knowledge for children. (p. 8)

The connections between topic, social interaction and type of talk are particularly fluid and dynamic in spoken exchanges, as speakers adjust what they say and how they say it according to the responses from others. Effective teaching of speaking and listening takes account of the ways these different factors bear on children's success in the main focus of any activity. (p. 10)

Quotations from government documents

Chapter 2

The characteristics of talk

In Chapter 1, I made the point that becoming an accomplished talker is as much concerned with social learning as with language learning. In other words, there is a social basis for the words we choose: we don't reinvent the wheel each time we carry out one of our 'talk purposes'. We come to understand how these tasks are managed from living, working and socialising in a number of different groups. Broadly speaking, we want to be accepted as members of these groups and so we absorb the group's ways of doing things even though we may each make adjustments according to our individual personalities.

Another way of putting this is to say that 'Language is not just a way of saying things – it's a way of behaving.' It's putting it too strongly to say that there are rules for carrying out each of the talk purposes, but there are expectations. Let me illustrate this by referring to a particular purpose for talk (the concepts of 'purpose', 'audience' and 'setting' are discussed in Chapter 1). Imagine that you want to invite someone to partake of a very British form of liquid refreshment. You will instinctively choose a form of words to carry out this task which you feel is appropriate for the audience and the setting.

Setting	Audience	Form of words
Charity garden party	Unknown members of the public	Can I offer you a cup of tea?
Kitchen table	Best friend	Cuppa?
Mother-in-law's house	Mother-in-law	Shall I put the kettle on?

I'm sure you can think of other choices which could be substituted for some of the above:

Can I?	*could become*	May I?
Cup of tea	*could become*	Liquid refreshment
		The cup that cheers
		Darjeeling or Earl Grey
Cuppa?	*could become*	Tea?
		Want some?
		You?

'Liquid refreshment' and 'the cup that cheers' are being used as synonyms, i.e. alternative words or phrases for 'tea'. They will probably only be used, if they are used at all nowadays, by people of a certain age (almost certainly 50+) and would be difficult to understand unless you are familiar with British culture of a certain era. Even British children might well not understand them. Ways of saying things change all the time – as you will be well aware if you live with teenagers! Using 'yesterday's word' for something marks you out as not belonging to that particular group.

As we move from one situation to another throughout the day, we all make adjustments to our style of speaking depending on our reading of the social situation. In today's society very formal spoken English is used in fewer and fewer situations. You might hear examples of it in a law court perhaps. I will use the word 'colloquial' to refer to those forms of spoken English which we use with people we encounter regularly but don't know intimately, and 'informal' to label the speech we might use when we are at our most relaxed, speaking with close friends, family and children. Do remember that these are only broad generalisations. There will be regional differences, perhaps gender differences and certainly, as I've already said, differences between the generations. There is no penalty for doing things in your own unique style although you might get some odd looks. You will see from the examples above that in formal English there is a preference for complete sentences; the vocabulary used tends to be more precise and nouns are preferred to pronouns.

The child's experience

There are pitfalls for young children in operating these social systems. They do not have the breadth of experience to understand always what is expected of them. An example I often quote is of a child who irritated his teacher by greeting her with 'Wotcher Miss!' when he arrived each morning. She expected 'Good morning Miss.' He was being friendly but she saw it as disrespectful.

The unfamiliar setting of school for a child just starting out is full of such potential pitfalls. Take, for example, a simple question: 'Would you like to put the books away for me, David.' David, perhaps more used to 'Put those books away NOW', may feel that 'No thanks' is a perfectly acceptable answer. It isn't. Situations like these need careful handling. Children can quickly be labelled as 'rude' or 'disrespectful' when what is needed is some fairly simple sharing of expectations or setting out of ground rules. Thankfully, I think the days are mainly over when teachers enhanced their power and status by deliberately using obscure forms of language. I remember working for a head teacher, years ago, who asked one small child: 'Tell me, Mitchell, what form did your misdemeanour take?' The child, who obviously hadn't a clue what he meant, answered 'Form two sir.' It seems to me that teaching assistants are in a good position to help children make adjustments to the language world of school – perhaps by gently explaining what the teacher expects or even by discussing with the children some of the ways things are said and done which they might not have come across before.

Spoken language structures

In the formal to informal range of expressions I illustrated above, there are some clear differences in the way the requests are structured. This is because when constructing sentences there *are* 'rules' – the rules of English syntax. Most people find just the mention of the word 'syntax' off-putting because it's part of the dreaded 'grammar' that we all feel we would rather avoid. In fact, we all know a lot of the rules of syntax. It's just that we have acquired this knowledge without being aware of it – and perhaps without knowing how to put into words what we know.

The syntax of spoken English

We might be inclined to think that speech is 'sloppier' or less carefully constructed than writing. Take the informal example I gave above: 'Cuppa?' What sort of sentence is that? Well actually, it isn't a sentence at all, though it is the remains of one. Unless we are in a rather formal setting, we frequently don't talk in whole sentences – to do so might mark us out as rather pompous or unfriendly. Instead we use what linguists call 'utterances'. A typical conversation might sound like this:

> A. How did it go at college today?
> B. Oh, not bad, thanks. Got a stack of work to do though.
> A. When for?
> B. Friday.

Imagine this written out as complete sentences. It would sound most peculiar:

> A. When does the work have to be completed by?
> B. It has to be completed by Friday.

Talk frequently takes place in face-to-face situations; for example if I raise the teapot in my right hand, look across to my friend and say 'You?' with a questioning inflection, she immediately understands that I am asking if she would like some tea. She doesn't need me to spell it out for her and might wonder why I was 'talking like a book' if I did so. At one time, children in some classrooms, if answering a question, were encouraged to answer always in complete sentences. This is often not how conversation works in the real world. Of course, we have all complained about the child who seems perpetually monosyllabic. I overheard a parent speaking on his mobile phone to a business associate: 'I won't give you my home phone number in case you encounter The Grunt.'

What is needed is an utterance that is appropriately structured for the situation. Most adults, if they are taking part in a group discussion or an argument, or telling a story, appreciate the need to be more explicit and will use more formal types of structuring conventions than those used when the talk is accompanying action or chatting with a group of friends. Children need to understand how to develop these more sustained forms of talk. This is part of 'learning to talk' and also 'learning about talk' mentioned on pp. 2–3.

Speech/writing contrasts

To generalise from the few examples above, speech and writing are rather different in their structures. Speech is not 'careless writing' – it has its own grammar, which is distinctive from the grammar of writing even though there are many overlaps. Sometimes, as we've seen already, speech moves closer to sounding like writing, such as a lecture delivered to an audience of several hundred people for example. The chances are that the lecturer will have prepared the speech carefully, perhaps rehearsed its delivery. She might have made copious notes or even written her text out in full. At the other extreme, speech and writing diverge widely in their structures. If you still feel doubtful about this, or guilty about the 'sloppy' way you or your family speak, try this experiment. Next time you respond to a suggestion, spell out your answer very carefully and completely:

> Would you like to go to the cinema tonight?
> Yes, I would like to go to the cinema tonight.

'OK' sounds friendlier, doesn't it? Or 'No thanks' or 'Sorry, I can't.' I don't think you need to have a full list of all the speech/writing differences, but below you will find some of the most noticeable ones.

In speaking, we often omit whole words, as in my example of 'Cuppa?' instead of 'Would you like a cup of tea?' Often it's the subject that is missed out, e.g. 'Coming for a walk?' instead of 'Are you coming for a walk?' The technical term for this is ellipsis.

Sometimes in speaking we slide over some of the sounds within a word, i.e. 'cuppa' instead of 'cup of'. This is known as elision and is quite natural, especially in the verb part of the sentence:

Could not	*becomes*	couldn't
He will	*becomes*	he'll

Unfortunately, this has led to some misunderstandings when it comes to writing out the fuller form of an utterance. For example, 'could've' is often written out fully as 'could of' when, of course, it should be 'could have'.

We often start to put an utterance together and then change our minds as we realise that our idea can be better expressed another way:

> I'm going to...I think I might go shopping this afternoon.

> The car...something's wrong with the brakes.

This is largely because speech is almost instantaneous and we don't have time to plan what we are going to say. If we were to write the above sentence, we would almost certainly write:

> Something seems to be wrong with the brakes on the car.

Something similar happens in a sentence like the one below:

> You know that bloke at the butcher's – he's emigrating to Australia.

Again, there's a restart here as the speaker first identifies the topic and then restates it using a pronoun: 'that bloke at the butcher's...he's...' If the sentence were to be written down it would probably be in the form of:

> The man in the butcher's is emigrating to Australia.

So I've made two changes: I've tidied up the syntax and I've changed 'bloke' to 'man'.

So far, I've highlighted the differences in syntax between speech and writing, but in the above example I introduced a vocabulary item. The slang form 'bloke' is more likely to be used in speech, though of course it will also crop up in informal writing. Some people talk about 'starting' something but feel that 'commence' is a more appropriate word for writing. I'm sure you can think of other examples. Non-specific nouns such as 'thingummy' and 'stuff' and phrases like 'sort of' and 'you know' help to soften informal conversation and make it less assertive.

There are a lot more 'fillers' in speech – 'ums', 'ers', 'well', 'you know' – that give the speaker time to think, to quickly scan a variety of words, for example, before choosing one:

> Which cake do you like best?
> I like ... er ... chocolate eclairs.

Writers have time to plan, cross out and start again but speakers must quickly scan all the possible relevant words and find the one that fits best.

Sometimes we want to signal that we haven't finished speaking – that we want to 'hold on to the conversational ball and not be interrupted'. As the DfES/QCA point out (2003a: 7), there is often competition to be the dominant voice. Participants in conversations have a tendency to jump in and finish each other's utterances:

> A. When I leave school I want to, you know, travel and, you know ...
> B. See the world a bit?

These 'ums' and 'ers' and 'you knows' are called hesitation phenomena. A certain number should be tolerated, especially from young and inexperienced speakers, but they can become irritating if there are too many of them.

Speakers can adjust their voices to help make their meanings clear or to signal a change of listener – perhaps one who commands greater respect. They can change such aspects as the pitch, the volume, the tone and the speed of their utterances. They can roar, whisper, cajole, nag and wheedle. They can use eye contact – or avoid it. They can pause dramatically. Some young people, especially perhaps boys, don't use the full range of possibilities much; this may be because they have a limited understanding of movement, gesture, position and their effects (DfES/QCA 2003a: 7). Or it may be just that they feel embarrassed and self-conscious. Drama and storytelling are good opportunities to encourage these aspects. I'll say more about how to help them with this in later chapters. Writers, of course, have none of the above opportunities to make their meanings more explicit other than by the means of punctuation and graphics:

> 'RRRRrrrrroar!!!!!' growled the tiger.

A good storyteller reading the above words can use volume, pitch and tone to very good effect here (see Chapters 4 and 5 for more about encouraging children's storytelling skills).

I've discussed at some length the differences between speech and writing because I think it's crucial to understanding how language work is planned and carried out in modern primary classrooms. Children need to be helped to understand that features of language, whether spoken or written, vary from one situation to another. It's most definitely not a case of 'One size fits all.'

To recap:

- There are differences between the structure of speech and the structure of writing.
- There are differences between formal, colloquial and informal speech structures.

All this may sound complicated, but try listening to a five-year-old playing in the home corner or the role-play area. He already knows that he has to change the way he speaks if he is pretending to be a teacher, a policeman, Dad being cross etc. What we need to do is to develop and extend this knowledge into a wider range of situations and therefore a wider 'repertoire' for the child of the kinds of language s/he feels comfortable with. I shall look more closely into exactly what this might involve in subsequent chapters.

Standard and non-standard English

We have looked at a range of formal to informal spoken language from which everyone – whether it's the Queen, you, me or Charlotte in Year 5 – will select in the course of a week or so. Admittedly, the demands on the Queen's spoken language must be very great, so that presumably she can employ a very wide range indeed, while Charlotte may still struggle when she is asked to speak in a whole-school assembly. There is, however, another range of choices which I need to draw attention to briefly. There is one kind of English, spoken and written, which is known as 'standard English' or 'the Queen's English.' Standard English (often referred to as SE) has been defined as:

> That variety of English which is usually used in print and which is normally taught in schools and to non-native speakers using the

language. It is also the variety which is normally used by educated people and used in news broadcasts and other similar situations. (LINC 1992: 355)

I'm sure you are familiar with the variety of English I'm talking about. It consists of a selection of grammar and vocabulary that is recognised and understood throughout the English-speaking world. The term 'standard English' does not, however, refer to the way in which the words are pronounced – more about that later.

The Queen, I presume, whether she is speaking formally or informally, always uses standard English. Charlotte in Year 5 may live in Glasgow, Norwich, Dudley or Bath. It is possible that for some of the time she uses a non-standard variety of spoken English, also sometimes referred to as a regional dialect, which is characterised by grammatical features and vocabulary typical of a particular geographical area. Sadly, many speakers who are conscious of regional elements in their speech still feel somehow inferior, as though standard English is the 'real' English and theirs is 'substandard'. To a linguist, SE is just another dialect of English – not a regional dialect but a social dialect. It's called a social dialect because it is associated with upper- and middle-class social groups particularly, but it affects everyone because of its official status.

It would be a mistake to assume that in this day and age non-standard dialects are completely different from SE. In the past, the differences were so great that people from one region would have had great difficulty understanding those from another. This is certainly not the case today. If anything, nowadays it is accent rather than dialect which causes difficulties in understanding (see below). It is possible that Charlotte in Year 5 may say something like:

Shall we put us coats on to go out to play, Miss?

but this expression is hardly likely to cause difficulties of comprehension for any teaching assistant hearing it – even one who does not come from Barnsley. There may very occasionally be some brief difficulties in understanding. When I spent my first Christmas term in a school in West Yorkshire, I was very puzzled when the head teacher, in assembly, asked the children to bring in some 'wassail cups'. Were we going to have a drunken

orgy? Sadly, no – this is the word in that region for Christmas tree decorations. In a note on the teaching of standard English in the National Curriculum document (DfEE/QCA 1999: 45), teachers are reminded that the three most common non-standard usages in England are:

- Subject–verb agreement (they was)
- Formation of past tense (have fell, I done)
- Formation of negatives (ain't)

In spite of examples like this, using standard English nowadays is largely a matter of prestige rather than of comprehension. The National Curriculum, however, makes it clear that all teachers must encourage children to use standard English (see quotes at the end of this chapter). This message is reinforced by defining progress in speaking as related to the ability to use standard English appropriately (DfES/QCA 2003a: 23).

Substandard forms of English

I have referred briefly to the long history of regional dialects, each of which originally had a very distinctive grammar and vocabulary. Sometimes the term 'non-standard English' is applied to language which does not have these historical roots, but which results from carelessness as, for example, 'I like them shoes you're wearing' or 'Them sort are my favourite.' The term 'non-standard' is used as a polite variant of 'substandard'.

Slang

Slang also lies outside this standard/non-standard dichotomy. Standard English speakers use slang and regions have slang terms familiar to those who live there. The term refers to ephemeral expressions, i.e. they come and go very quickly, more often used in speech than in writing. They are indicative of those who use them being members of various groups, possibly age groups, social groups or groups who spend a lot of time together in shared activities. As I write, 'bling' is a word that is being used by my students – and others – to refer to expensive jewellery but by the time you come to read this, the term may have disappeared for ever.

Received pronunciation

As I hope I have made clear, the term 'standard English' refers to a particular selection of grammar and vocabulary which has no specific regional links. It is possible to speak it with a Yorkshire accent or a Somerset accent – or an American or Australian accent – although the standard English used in America and Australia differs from standard British English. But just as standard English is a high-prestige variant and usage of it tends to be associated with power and status, so there is an accent, known as received pronunciation (RP), which has no regional connotations and is associated with, for example, BBC newsreaders (or used to be – these days, the national news is sometimes read in a Welsh accent although it is unusual to hear a 'Brummie' accent). It's possible that some readers may associate RP with adjectives such as 'posh' or 'plummy'. It sometimes produces a 'Who does she think she is?' reaction. Whereas the National Curriculum requires schools to introduce SE if it's believed that the children are not already using it, and to promote its use, there is no requirement to encourage children to use this accent. In fact, the number of people who speak RP or something close to it is much smaller than the number of speakers of standard English.

I believe that discussion of standard English and its use needs careful and tactful handling in schools. Criticisms of the child's vocabulary and grammar are by implication criticisms of the child's home. There are two ways of tackling the issue. One is by adult modelling of standard English. It's likely that most adults in the classroom will use this form of English most of the time, with perhaps a few regional variations thrown in (such as the 'wassail cups' example above). Children are also constantly exposed to examples on films and videos and in their reading. They will, to a certain extent, make their own decisions about how far to emulate these models.

Secondly we come back to the point I made in Chapter 1 about the need for children to learn *about* language. There should be plenty of opportunities, especially at Key Stage 2, for children to talk about similarities and differences in the ways in which we talk to each other – because of our different jobs, the places in which we live or because we are sad or angry etc. This is reinforced by the DfES/QCA by pointing out that progress in speaking and listening is 'related to children's ability to talk explicitly about speaking and listening' (2003a: 23).

Drama is an excellent opportunity for opening up such discussions – whether it's something the children have watched or something they have taken part in. Similarly, they need to be made aware that language is changing all the time – although slang terms are often very short-lived, even the 'official' language that seems to have existed for ever is actually very different from that which their parents and grandparents learned at school. This could be an interesting starting point for some first-hand research and data gathering. The more we can interest children in language, the less frightened of it they will be – it should be something to find out about and enjoy rather than the 'monster grammar' or the 'demon spelling' waiting to trap the unwary.

Summary

In this chapter I have looked at:

- The formal to informal continuum of language variation.
- The structure of spoken English and some of the ways in which it differs from the structure of written English.
- Standard and non-standard English.
- Substandard English and slang.
- Received pronunciation.

Further reading

DfEE/QCA (1999) *The National Curriculum: Handbook for Primary Teachers in England.* London: DfEE/QCA.

DfEE/QCA (2000) *Curriculum Guidance for the Foundation Stage.* London: DfEE/QCA.

DfES/QCA (2003a) *Speaking, Listening and Learning: Working with Children in Key Stages 1 and 2. Handbook.* London: DfES/QCA.

DfES/QCA (2003b) *Speaking, Listening and Learning: Working with Children in Key Stages 1 and 2. Teaching Objectives and Classroom Activities.* London: DfES/QCA.

LINC (1992) *Language in the National Curriculum: Materials for Professional Development.* (Obtainable from: LINC Secretary,

Department of English Studies, University of Nottingham, Nottingham NG7 7RO.)

Whitehead, M. (1997) *Language and Literacy in the Early Years.* London: Paul Chapman (esp. Ch. 3).

Wilson, A. (2001) *Language Knowledge for Primary Teachers.* London: David Fulton Publishers (esp. Ch. 6).

***Curriculum Guidance for the Foundation Stage* (DfEE/QCA 2000)**
Practitioners should give particular attention to providing opportunities for children to communicate thoughts, ideas and feelings and build up relationships with adults and each other. (p. 44)

***National Curriculum: Programme of Study for Speaking and Listening* (DfEE/QCA 1999)**

Key Stage 1 (pp. 44–5)
To speak clearly, fluently and confidently to different people, pupils should be taught to:
a)   speak with clear diction and appropriate intonation
b)   choose words with precision
c)   organise what they say
To join in as members of a group, pupils should be taught to:
a)   take turns in speaking
b)   relate their contributions to what has gone on before
Pupils should be introduced to some of the main forms of spoken standard English and be taught to use them.

Key Stage 2 (pp. 50–2)
To speak with confidence in a range of contexts, adapting their speech for a range of purposes and audiences, pupils should be taught to:
a)   use vocabulary and syntax that enables them to communicate more complex meanings
b)   gain and maintain the response of different audiences
To talk effectively as members of a group, pupils should be taught to:
a)   vary contributions to suit the activity and purpose, including exploratory and tentative comments where ideas are being

collected together, and reasoned, evaluative comments as discussion moves to conclusions or actions

b) take up and sustain different roles, adapting them to suit their situation, including chair, scribe and spokesperson

c) deal politely with opposing points of view and enable discussion to move on.

Pupils should be taught the grammatical constructions that are characteristic of spoken standard English and to apply this knowledge appropriately in a range of contexts.

Speaking, Listening and Learning: Working with Children in Key Stages 1 and 2 (DfES/QCA 2003a)

There are features of language that are distinctively oral and do not occur in written form . . . There are also distinctive forms used in talk, particularly spoken standard English, which clearly differ from the written form . . . the interactive nature of talk and its ephemeral nature are in direct contrast to most writing . . . the curriculum for speaking and listening must . . . give due weight to the distinctiveness of talk. (p. 7)

Non-verbal communication is integral to talk and obviously supplements – or subverts – the spoken word. Many children have a limited understanding of movement, gesture, position and their effects. (p. 7)

Quotations from government documents

Chapter 3

Learning to talk, 0–4 years

We hear a lot of concern expressed these days about children who are starting school 'with no language'. In fact, these anxieties are not new – they have been uttered in some form or other ever since all children were given free access to state education. The truth is that most children – with the exception of those who have a high degree of handicap, a gross defect of intelligence or a severe impairment of hearing – have learned a great deal of language before they are five years old.

It is true that they may not have learned the language that we as educators want or expect them to have. Many children are not familiar with traditional nursery rhymes and stories but they may be able to tell us a great deal about TV programmes or films – a four-year-old recently described to me with great enthusiasm the saga of *Thunderbirds*. I have the feeling that he might not be so enthusiastic about *Little Red Riding Hood*. We must be careful – adults are notoriously sentimental when it comes to sharing songs and stories with children. Phrases such as 'modern rubbish' and 'I loved it, so why doesn't he?' come uneasily to mind.

Before we jump to conclusions about children's language abilities, it's important to remember what was said about settings in Chapter 1. Some children who appear to be chatterboxes at home may not feel confident speaking within the context of the classroom as they perceive it. The purposes for talk seem so different from home, the most dramatic difference being the larger audience and competition for the adult's attention.

Children from less privileged socio-economic backgrounds have been particularly susceptible to criticism. But is this fair? In homes where both parents have highly paid jobs, it's possible that neither Mum nor Dad may have much time to talk to their children. Even the so-called advantages of the affluent home may militate against good language development – their own room with a television or a computer separates children from the flow of talk which is so necessary if their language is to progress. It is likely that there is as much contrast in children's language abilities within each social class as there is between the classes.

Research suggests that *all* children between their first and fifth birthdays seem to acquire language in the same sort of way. By the age of five, they can use talk to achieve a range of purposes including:

- Asking questions.
- Recalling past events.
- Commenting on the world around them.
- Stating intentions or desires.

To do all of the above requires a fairly extensive knowledge of syntax including knowledge of:

- *How to formulate questions in a variety of ways.* This is trickier than you might think. Even 'When are we going to the park?' requires choice of the appropriate question word and inversion of the verb: 'are we' not 'we are'. Added to this is the questioning intonation. All of this knowledge will be gained in gradual stages, of course.
- *How to form past tenses.* See page 32 for more on this.
- *How to phrase requests so that they are likely to get what they want.* This might involve a use of a conditional, as in 'If you've finished the washing-up, Mummy, can we...?' In other words, expressing the hope that something might happen provided other things happen. It's not only the grammar that's impressive here, but the realisation that the choice of words and the order of the words might make a difference to the outcome. There is also likely to be an appropriate choice of tone and perhaps gesture.

Vocabulary

Each child has a vocabulary of several thousand words which will be influenced by the interests and concerns of those around them. For example, children who live on farms will know a lot of words linked to farm implements, including being able to distinguish between different types of tractor. The same is likely to be true of children whose families are involved with boats or cars, computers, golf or football and so on. Many concepts will develop slowly, e.g. words for large groups of things and words which specify the members of groups such as 'flower' and 'daffodil'.

There's much more to words, however, than just labelling items. Think of a word such as 'gone'. Children learn that sometimes it applies to things that only happen once:

> The bath water has gone. (And it won't come back.)

Sometimes it applies to things that happen regularly:

> Mummy has gone to work. (Most children are reasonably sure that she's likely to come back.)

Children quickly begin to understand some everyday uses of metaphor – for example, that 'I'm boiling hot' is not the same as 'The kettle's boiling.' We expect abstract concepts like 'good' and 'naughty' to be understood by five-year-olds although I'm sure their understanding of these terms is often different from that of adults.

Talk accompanying action

In the very earliest months, the purposes for talk that the child encounters largely involve the business of everyday life: bathing, dressing, meals, outings to the shops etc. The words and utterances are likely to come up regularly at more or less the same points in every day and they are easy to grasp because they accompany actions:

> Shall we tie your shoelaces?
>
> Would you like some more milk?
>
> Time for your bath.
>
> How about a story?

Gradually, after much repetition, the children will begin to take over the words for themselves, though at first they will reduce the utterance to only one or two key words, e.g. 'Tie shoelace' or 'More milk.'

It would be a mistake, however, to think that language is only acquired in the context of eating, washing, dressing and the other daily necessities of childhood existence. Children observe – and are involved in – many aspects of adult life and most of these are rich in opportunities for language learning. Seventeen-month-old Rory was out in the car with his mother when they stopped at the traffic lights. 'Green – that means go!' she told him as the lights changed. All that day she heard him saying to himself 'Go, go, go!' Some time later, he picked up the green lid of his drinking cup and said 'Go!' and was even heard to say the word as he ate some lettuce. With adult feedback and more opportunities to observe, the language learning and the social learning will both develop until when green means 'go' and when not will become clearer.

Of course, refining and clarifying the learning of concepts and their application in the real world doesn't stop at the age of five – it continues throughout life. Your job as a teaching assistant should provide you with many opportunities to support children as they experiment with using a new word or try to find expression for a new idea. Sometimes it's all too easy to be struck by what children don't know and can't do. We need to constantly remind ourselves that they have already coped with some amazingly sophisticated language learning without any direct instruction or specific 'language lessons'. What's even more impressive is that some children can do all this in more than one language.

How do babies learn to talk?

This is a complex subject and one on which researchers are divided on. It might be tempting to think that children are like budgerigars or parrots, learning to talk simply by imitating those around them. I need to be careful here – *The Times* has reported the story of a parrot in New York, speaking with a broad Bronx accent, which is apparently capable of generating new conversation. If this is true, the bird must have a grasp of grammar – the system of rules for combining words to make new utterances. No one has ever suggested that parrots are capable of this before. Children, on the other hand, are quite clearly capable of saying things that they have never heard an adult say.

Children's innate abilities

Children do copy those around them, of course. We saw the link Rory made between the word 'go' and a green traffic light, but he quickly began to apply his new-found knowledge in ways that an adult would not, i.e. saying 'go' as he drank from his green cup and ate his lettuce. Even more amazing is the fact that children seem able to learn the grammatical systems of their language and use these systems to form new sentences. We know this because we can see them over-applying the rules of syntax in ways that a native adult speaker would never do, the formulation of the past tense being a case in point. Usually, when conjugating regular English verbs, the past tense is formed by adding 'ed' to the base form.

- climb   climb**ed**
- talk   talk**ed**
- want   wan**ted**

There are, however, a good many irregular past tense forms. For example:

- go   went
- eat   ate
- run   ran
- fly   flew

These take time to learn and in the meantime we sometimes hear children create utterances such as:

> They seed the International Rescue coming.

> Trudy knowed that because Mummy telled it to her.

Examples such as this suggest that the capacity to learn language is an innate part of a child's genetically transmitted inheritance, like walking upright or using the hands as tools. An American linguist, Noam Chomsky, drew attention to this explanation as to how we learn language. He suggested that inside each of our brains is something called a language acquisition device (LAD). By this he means that we each have parts of our brains which have the ability to process speech, i.e. we can represent a range of meanings to each other symbolically and in the kinds of patterns which we call the grammar of a language.

LAD is no use without LASS

The ability to speak and to understand language may well be innate but we wouldn't use these abilities if we were not living in groups – or in the case of babies, unless someone else was continually urging us to respond and to share in meaning-making. Adults, in their interactions with children, continually offer them new evidence of how things are done, starting immediately the baby is born by holding the child in a face-to-face position and 'talking' to him as if he understood – even pausing for him to make a 'reply'. And children incorporate what is offered to them into their own developing language systems. At first, they make sounds – and all babies make the same sounds regardless of the language going on around them. But only the sounds which the adults recognise receive a positive response, so gradually the other sounds are dropped from the baby's repertoire. The next stage is that the baby says something which the adult recognises as a word, and then another, and language develops rapidly from that point. The children make errors in the sense that they say things the adult does not recognise as part of the 'mature' system, and then new evidence is provided which enables the developing speakers to modify their original hypotheses.

Another aspect of the adult's role is to act as provider of those regular opportunities to hear and respond to speech – in similar forms every day – which I referred to above. Familiar routines and settings, with carefully prepared slots into which children can make their inputs, are crucial aspects of language development. Jerome Bruner refers to the help children get from their families and communities as a Language Acquisition Support System. In your role as a teaching assistant, especially in the Foundation Stage, you will still be a vital part of this support system. In Chapter 4 I will look more specifically at some of the kinds of help you can provide – assuming responsibility for some of the parental roles while the child is in nursery and school – and using the opportunities provided by those contexts to extend the child's language repertoire.

Summary

In this chapter I have looked at:

- The knowledge about language that children are likely to have acquired before the Foundation Stage.
- The purposes for which very young children use language.
- Their knowledge of vocabulary and syntax.
- The role of adults in supporting language learning at this stage.

Further reading

Whitehead, M. (1997) *Language and Literacy in the Early Years.* London: Paul Chapman (esp. Ch. 3).

Wilson, A. (2001) *Language Knowledge for Primary Teachers.* London: David Fulton Publishers (esp. Ch. 3).

Chapter 4

Talking and learning in the Foundation Stage

The rest of this book is devoted to describing some of the ways schools can plan to take children forward as speakers and listeners. Before I begin to discuss age-specific concerns, I will set out some general attitudes and values with regard to talk that should be found in the school as a whole.

A whole-school approach to talk

In order to develop children as confident speakers and listeners, a school must demonstrate:

- A commitment to involving children actively in their learning.
- Awareness of the range of talk activities that the school can promote. During these activities everyone should be clear that speaking and listening is a main, if not *the*, focus of the activity. There should, if appropriate, be a speaking and listening outcome such as a prepared talk or a reading.
- Rigorous standards in adhering to structures and deadlines so that time is not wasted and talk is purposeful.
- Commitment to helping children to reflect explicitly on what they know, understand and can do.
- Awareness of what it means to develop children as talkers – skills such as talking for a wide range of purposes and audiences, using appropriate genres and registers, using appropriate intonation and emphasis, summarising, adapting to someone else's point of view.
- Commitment to a collaborative ethos throughout the school in all areas including discipline and decision-making.

- Commitment to non-sexist and non-racist language.
- Recognition of the teacher's role in developing speaking and listening.
- Effective monitoring and assessment procedures for speaking and listening.
- Sensitivity to the child's community and social group.

Each of the above is equally important regardless of the key stage or age of the child. Expectations and emphases will vary considerably, however, as the child moves through the school. Let's look first at concerns specific to children aged 3–5.

The move from home to school

Tizard and Hughes (1986) express some useful warnings. Their observations of children at home showed them displaying a range of interests and skills which enabled them to be powerful learners. Yet observations of the same children at school showed a fundamental lack of awareness by the nursery staff of these skills and interests – the children appeared to be much less active thinkers in the nursery school situation than at home. It is probably true that today's children have more extended contacts with a range of adults than was the case 20 years ago, but not all those adults are sympathetic to their conversational needs. As Tizard and Hughes point out:

> A big obstacle to the integration of the two worlds of home and school in the pre-school years is the young child's relatively poorly developed communication skills. It is difficult even for the more articulate children to communicate about home when at school, and about school when at home. They frequently make incorrect assumptions about what the person they are talking about knows about their other life and what they would need to know in order to understand them. An important task for the nursery school is to help children improve these communications skills. (Tizard and Hughes 1986: 265)

Bridging the home/school gap

As a teaching assistant you can play a vital role in helping children to come to terms with the expectations of the nursery or foundation classroom. This might occasionally involve you in working with the whole class, but probably more often with a group or an individual child. In the following respects you are more or less taking over from the role of a supportive parent:

● *Have one-to-one conversations with a child whenever possible.* All the research suggests that one-to-one or small group conversations are the most helpful for children aged 3–5. This kind of conversation is extremely difficult for a busy teacher to replicate for more than a few seconds at a time.

● *Show awareness of and respect for all the children's languages.* Some children will have the advantage of speaking more than one language. If it is possible for you or a colleague to hold one-to-one or group conversations in the child's home language, this is very supportive.

● *Talk about topics of interest and concern to the child.* In an encouraging home environment a child will often ask questions or initiate topics of conversation. This happens less frequently in a busy classroom. A quiet child can be encouraged by a statement rather than a question: 'I have a cat like that at home' is more likely to offer the child a conversational opening, if needed, than 'Is that a picture of your cat?'

● *Encourage the child to share an interest with you in an object or an event.* Here perhaps you may have opportunities to extend as well as to confirm shared interests: try to range widely over all kinds of shared experience. Obviously a detailed knowledge of the group you are working with is essential – pets, holidays, new babies, arrivals and departures of all kinds are just some of the likely topics. It's also important to help your little group to understand what's going on in the rest of the school – explain to them about a fund-raising activity for instance, which they might have heard mentioned in assembly but may be very unclear about.

● *Try to pay attention to the way the child is looking at things – to 'get on their wave length'.* This can be more difficult than it sounds. Gordon Wells expresses it particularly well:

Talking with young children is very much like playing at ball with them. What the adult has to do for this game to be successful is first ensure that the child is ready, with arms cupped, to catch the ball. Then the ball must be thrown gently and accurately so that it lands squarely in the child's arms. When it is the child's turn to throw, the adult must be prepared to run wherever it goes and bring it back to where the child really intended it to go. (Wells 1987: 50)

- *Compensate for the child's language limitations.* This is part of what Wells is saying in the above quote. For children to play their part effectively in conversation we need to adjust our utterances so that they can make sense of them.
- *Use exaggerated intonation if you feel it would be helpful.*
- *Emphasise key words.* Everyday speech is rapid and easy to lose track of – as I know to my cost when I try out my schoolgirl French on anything more complicated than buying a kilo of potatoes. Slow it down and make sure the 'content words' – the ones that carry the meaning – come across clearly. This will be particularly helpful for speakers of English as an additional language.
- *Make a special effort to listen.* Use all the context cues you have and your knowledge about the child to 'fill out' the scarce verbal cues the child may be offering. Check to see you have understood correctly – adults sometimes are too quick to assume they've got it right which can be very frustrating for the child!
- *Don't be too didactic (i.e. 'teacherly').* It's a burden for the child and will discourage them from speaking to you if you try to turn every occasion into a language lesson.
- *Accept the child's way of putting things, at least to begin with.* Families vary considerably (as I discussed in Chapter 2) in their expectations of their children as talkers. There are differences as to what gets talked about and how it is talked about. Children need patient help and guidance in adapting to the expectations of the school and the teacher in ways that don't seem to undervalue how things are done in their homes. You may be a parent of a child in the school or you may have the opportunity to liaise with parent helpers or other members of the local

community involved in voluntary work in the school. All of that is very helpful.

Explain the school to the child

Still with an emphasis on bridging the home/school gap, here are some issues and topics that could be the basis of fruitful discussions.

The distribution and organisation of time

- Quite young children these days are expected to sit on the carpet for up to 20 minutes or half an hour – perhaps as part of the literacy hour. There will be extended periods of listening and there is an expectation that the child will remain 'switched on' during the whole session, i.e. be alert and ready to participate at all times. As I have already said, whole-class sessions may be particularly difficult for children who are accustomed to having the speaking directed at them much more specifically, with some accompanying eye contact and facial expressions. Now, the teacher expects them to answer even if she seems to be looking at someone else. You will probably find that together with the teacher you can easily compile a daily list of children who need special help during those carpet sessions to help them stay focused – even if it's just something as simple as arranging that they sit near you during the session.

- Time is much more tightly parcelled up and structured than it is at home. No sooner is one thing over than something else starts – perhaps in a different place. Just talking this over with newcomers and taking them on a guided tour of the different areas is helpful. Later on, they could assume this role for even newer pupils, giving the more experienced ones that sense of being 'the expert' which is vital to building their confidence as speakers.

- Perhaps even more difficult to handle are the sessions of child-initiated activities which most schools still incorporate into the day at the Foundation Stage. During these periods, which have a prescribed beginning and end, the child is expected to be busy the whole time. In some schools the child will be expected to produce a plan of some kind, perhaps an oral plan, for the time available and will have to give an account at the end of what s/he has done. Again, careful observation will quickly indicate those children who need guidance or help.

One difficulty for the child may be having to compete for resources or negotiate for a turn at an activity which is very popular. It may be necessary to do another 'second best' activity until the more popular activity becomes free. Of course, there will be children who can't deal with that, and an argument or even a fight may break out. Your intervention can help the children to decide what they will do to calm down. Later on, talking through problems which arose during the day is another way of showing commitment to making the children active, reflective learners and members of the community of the classroom.

The behaviour expected in lessons

- Putting your hand up when you want to say something may come as second nature to anyone who's used to schools, but it's not something that happens at home. Some children have a knack of getting themselves noticed while others find it very difficult. As part of a research project, I watched one poor girl for three days. She frequently put her hand up but not once was she asked to contribute. Yet when I spoke to her afterwards she had valid and interesting things to say. There are many reasons why this happens. There may be gender issues: do the boys in the class get more of the teacher's attention than the girls? Is there a particular person or group who is continually focused on? Teachers can sometimes be quite unaware that this is happening and it's useful to have an observer who can look at the discussions objectively and report on the number and quality of the children's contributions.

- What might become apparent is that some children are not responding well to indirect invitations to speak such as 'Well now!' or 'Let's see who are the clever children in this class!' Also, some children may be unsure about whether they said the right thing – again, the feedback can sometimes be ambiguous. You can offer praise and reassurance.

- There are some quite subtle distinctions to be learned: for example, 'Would you like to pick up that piece of paper for me?' is not at all the same as 'Would you like a piece of cake at playtime?'

● As a teaching assistant you can play a valuable role in the 'grooming' of the children as classroom talkers which is a vital part of these early years. You can offer reminders such as 'What have we said about not shouting out?' or 'Put your hand up if you know the answer' to those who need them.

Working in groups

● 'Talk partners' have become a regular part of some classrooms. 'Turn to the person next to you and tell each other what you like best/decide how you will help Little Bo-Peep/write the correct answer on your whiteboard' and so on. As before, your role here would be to watch and see how these interactions are progressing. Are the pairings appropriate? Are some children inclined to give an answer themselves rather than discuss it with their partner? Are some pairs sitting in silence? Would the behaviour in the classroom be improved if some pairings were changed?

● Some of these problems are exacerbated in groups larger than two, and many children will need help in 'becoming a good group member' – some adults have never learned how to do it. Don't just be on the lookout for problems, of course; even at a very young age, some children have surprisingly good group skills and it's useful, in the assessment of speaking and listening, to be able to make on-the-spot observations which can be entered later onto more formal talk assessment sheets (see Chapter 7).

● It's a good idea to vary the pairs or groups that include children for whom English is an additional language (EAL). They need to observe and participate in the conversation in English and they will be enormously supported by working with English-speaking children. But sometimes working with a child who speaks the same home language will help them to consolidate their ideas and develop their confidence.

Explaining procedures and introducing appropriate vocabulary

This harks back to the familiarisation processes mentioned earlier – taking the newly arrived children on a guided tour of the facilities etc.

Words such as 'assembly' and 'cloakroom' and 'calling the register' are all meaningless jargon to some children. Calling it what? 'Play dough' perhaps and 'Clixi' or even 'maths', 'literacy' or 'PE' might be unfamiliar terms. Even a Year 5 child was heard to ask what 'PE' stood for. 'Is it "physical exercise"?' he asked. No one knew for certain and there was a vigorous debate. Some of these terms are explained – perhaps once, but never again – while others are taken for granted. It's not a question of bad teaching but just the numbers of people involved, the speed at which things happen and the habit some children have of going off into a parallel universe at the crucial moment when something is being explained. Some children may never have had to tell anyone what they wanted on their plate at lunchtime. 'Baked beans, Sunshine?' might result in something you absolutely hate being piled up on the plate in front of you, if you're not quick enough. Of course, even teaching assistants have to take a break sometimes and I'm not suggesting that you should be eternally vigilant – just that there are needs and opportunities for one-to-one explanations of the most basic kind.

Using the home corner/role-play areas etc.

Almost all foundation classrooms offer opportunities to try out going to the hairdresser's, hiding in the witch's cave or Little Bear's Den etc. Some children will have had experience of role play at home, but for others the uses of language they have been exposed to will be much more literal and they will need help in the 'Let's pretend' functions of language. For all of them, role play can be enriched when an adult joins in sensitively (see pp. 54–5 for more about this topic).

Discussing a story

Just as some children will have shared role-play games with their families, some will have shared stories. Some will be used to discussing the stories too; some will not. There is a vocabulary for talking about stories (see pp. 49–50).

◼ **Extending the opportunities for talk in the Foundation Stage**

There are so many of these that all I can do here is to try to suggest some of the opportunities for which you and the teacher will want to plan. If you have read Chapter 1 you will remember my three categories of:

Purpose   Audience   Setting

The most important thing to bear in mind when planning a 'talk curriculum' is to give the children something interesting to talk about (a purpose). It's tempting to put 'increasing the children's vocabulary' at the top of the agenda, but I would argue that 'making new meanings' should take the top position. As the children become immersed in the situation, perhaps also meeting new audiences, maybe in new settings, then new words will be introduced to them. You can help them to make these words their own. And it's not just new words, but new ways of 'behaving' linguistically (as I explained in Chapter 1). This could be represented as:

NEW CONTEXT CREATED
↓
NEW ROLES ESTABLISHED
↓
NEW RELATIONSHIP IN OPERATION
↓
NEW LANGUAGE DEMANDS MADE
↓
LANGUAGE DEMANDS TACKLED
↓
LANGUAGE DEVELOPMENT

Each conversation will be unique but it is likely that certain activities will give rise to talk for certain purposes. The word 'role' may suggest drama or 'role play' and I shall have something to say about those later, but here I would like to focus on more general roles: the child as interviewer, the child as guide to the school, as expert in how to look after a pet rabbit and so on.

The role of the teaching assistant

I will give some indication in each of the following activities of what your specific role in them might be, but as a general rule, each of the following is very important at this stage:

- Being a model for the kinds of things that are said and how to say them.
- Encouraging the children to interact confidently with other children and with a range of adults.
- Listening carefully and responding to what the children have to say – putting them in control as much as possible.
- Encouraging children to expand on their comments and answers.

Links with the community and the outside world

Links with the children's homes have already been emphasised so it seems sensible to start by offering some comments on ways in which schools extend the range of adults in the community the children come into contact with.

The 'owl person'

This might equally be someone who has some chickens about to hatch out or someone who trains guide dogs for the blind or deaf, i.e. any member of the community who is invited into school to demonstrate something to the children – a mother bathing a baby would be another example. Some of the visitors should be fluent speakers in the other languages spoken in the school.

Before the visit
The visit will probably be part of planned work by the teacher, perhaps a science project, with all sorts of opportunities for spoken and written language as well. As preparation before the visit, you may want to discuss in a small group the information already given by the teacher to the whole class and help the children to speculate on what they are going to see:

I wonder what...?

How do you think that...?

We must remember to ask whether...?

Children can be encouraged to think of things they would like to ask the visitor and to form questions that can feasibly be answered. Other questions should not, of course, be discouraged – such as 'What will the owl think of our classroom?' – but it needs to be gently pointed out that it's really impossible ever to know what owls think. Questioning is quite a tricky form of speaking, especially when under pressure of time. We have all probably found ourselves unable to form a suitable question immediately after hearing someone give a talk though in the car on the way home they come easily to mind.

During the visit

It may well be that the excitement of the event renders the children silent. There is also the issue of the older, perhaps unfamiliar, person as audience (see Chapter 1). You may need to prompt them by recalling the discussion you had with them:

Adam had an interesting question he wanted to ask you about. (But leave Adam to explain his question for himself if he can!)

Watch out for children who ask follow-up questions that prove that they have listened to and assimilated what has been said. Praise those who develop something said or asked by another child.

Encourage good social skills – saying hello and goodbye to the visitor, perhaps showing him or her out, or explaining what happens when the bell goes.

After the visit

This is when your skills as an effective listener should really come into play. If possible, give the children a follow-up activity that will encourage them to reflect on what has happened. In the case of the owl person's visit, they might help you to dissect an owl pellet which would give you the opportunity to reinforce some of the 'owl' vocabulary and perhaps introduce more. If chickens have been left to hatch out in the classroom, you and the children can devise a daily chart. The children can decide with you how to record progress of the eggs. On other occasions, some role play might be an appropriate follow-up activity or a child could tell a small group how she looks after her pet (either real or imaginary).

Hopefully you will gain an insight into what the children thought about and learned from the occasion and how it has shaped their understandings.

Talking about talk

As well as helping the children to explore a new experience orally, try to help them to become reflective about the talk itself. The teacher might have established a 'talk wall' in the classroom in which case you and the children could write up:

- Some good examples of the questions that were asked.
- Interesting technical terms.
- Interesting words that the children came up with – these might even be invented words to describe the sounds the owl made, for example.

This is a good opportunity to draw the children's attention to the range of languages spoken in the class and to include some of the owl words in other languages.

Out-of-school visits

At this stage, this will probably be something fairly simple and straightforward such as a walk to the shops, the park or the library. The change to an out-of-school setting may well encourage some children who are usually quiet in the classroom to chat to you more freely. There are many opportunities for child-initiated topics. Children will be able to make links with their out-of-school lives: 'I come here with my dad' or 'That's where my granny lives.' There are also many opportunities for discussing and explaining examples of environmental print: 'What is this notice telling us?' or 'How do I know which is the way in?' for example. Notice the range of questions the children are asking – especially those who are asking the more searching 'Why' or 'How' questions. How can you encourage a more extensive and wider range of questions next time you go out?

Sharing and discussing a story

The storytelling space

I have already discussed settings and the influence they have on talk but nowhere is this more important than during story-sharing sessions. Having a comfortable area to work in makes all the difference, especially if you can use the same area on a regular basis so that the children associate it with storytelling. Some classrooms already have reading areas with comfy chairs or cushions but if your classroom doesn't have this facility it might be possible to set one up.

When you are sharing a story, it's very important to position the children carefully so that everyone can see you and each other. You need to remove any irrelevant objects that the children might be tempted to fiddle with.

To read or to tell?

If you are not very experienced, you may prefer to have a book to read from. Nowadays there are lots of large format books which are ideal for sharing with a group, especially if you have some way of propping up the book securely. Apart from providing a sense of security it also enables you to enjoy the pictures with the children and to talk about some aspects of the text – the shape of a letter or a spelling pattern perhaps (for more on this see *Supporting Reading* in this series).

The great thing about telling a story, as distinct from reading it, is that it enables you to have more eye contact with the children and to present the story to them in a much more powerful way than if you are concerned about losing your place or getting the words right. This may seem a terrifying prospect if you've never done it, but with a little practice (possibly into a tape recorder or even in front of a mirror!) you really will find it becomes easier. You'll probably find that you need to tell a story three times before you feel ownership of it – then you can start changing it a bit, developing your favourite part or putting slightly different words into the mouth of a character to suit yourself or your audience. Sometimes, of course, the children don't want that – they have a favourite version that they want to hear time and again. But it's good to have a range of possibilities at your fingertips (for further help and advice on storytelling, see the books listed at the end of this chapter). It's like learning to ride a bike – it is best to just get on with it and have a go.

Funny voices and regional accents

Some people are good at these and they can significantly enhance a story whether you're reading it or telling it. But don't be put off if this is not your forte. What is important is to help the children, who are just beginning to explore the world of narrative at this stage, to distinguish between the narrator's voice and the voices of the characters. You can do this even in a quite simple way – perhaps just by varying the volume or pitch of your voice. For example, after a visit such as I described earlier from an owl person, you and the teacher might decide to share *Owl Babies* by Martin Waddell with the class. There are three baby owls, the mummy owl and a storyteller whose voices we hear and it would be quite simple to come up with a voice for each of them.

More dramatic readings may come in time, especially if, as suggested above, you tell your favourite stories over and over again until you feel you have ownership of them.

Focusing attention: using a prop

Children at this stage are not good at sitting still and listening for long periods. One way of holding their attention is to have an object associated with the story – perhaps a fluffy toy owl if you are reading *Owl Babies*. Again, telling rather than reading makes it easier to hold and use your object as part of the story session. Some schools have a collection of storysacks to accompany some of their storybooks. These contain replicas of the main characters made from felt or other materials, together with tapes, games and other related activities. Originally the brainchild of Neil Griffiths, his storysacks are available for sale (see 'Further reading' at the end of this chapter) or you could get together with others to make some storysacks. A simpler option is to create characters from your story by drawing faces on brown paper bags with felt pens. Other related objects can be bought cheaply at car boot sales etc. Once they are familiar with a story, children can be encouraged to retell it themselves, using the puppets or the objects. This is an excellent way of encouraging them to structure longer sequences of talk and you can introduce linking words such as 'next', 'after that', 'the last thing', 'first, second' and so on.

More ideas for helping to develop listening skills

- Another good way of maintaining attention is to encourage the children to join in the reading or telling. They might do some simple actions or they can say the words with you. If they know what's coming they can, either individually or in groups, say the words spoken by one of the characters or just tell you what's coming next over the page. It's very helpful for EAL speakers and non-readers/beginning readers if you choose a text with a pattern – some repetition – so that the children can memorise the words. It isn't 'reading' but it's a step on the way to becoming a reader and makes children feel more confident about them-selves as readers (for more on this see *Supporting Reading* in this series, p. 68). Whatever you do, don't allow the children to read in the 'Dalek' voices which they sometimes adopt when reading aloud to the teacher. This comes about when children are decoding the text word by word and not thinking about the overall meaning of what they are saying. Encourage them to vary the volume and pitch of their voices, depend-ing on the meaning of the words.

- You might like to give the children the opportunity to 'talk to the char-acters' in the story and perhaps ask them some questions. You could use the paper bag puppets or the characters in the storysack for this – or you could try going into role yourself. This need not involve great acting skills – children are very accepting at this stage! You could go straight into role or you could say something like 'I'm going to stand up and walk to the door, and when I come back, I shall be the mummy owl [or ...] and you can ask me some questions.' As already mentioned, sometimes making a statement gets the ball rolling faster. As you sit down you could say something like 'My poor little Percy [one of the baby owls] was so upset last night. Can you guess why?' If it's appro-priate you might introduce a simple prop – a hat or a scarf or a bag of some kind. Bags are intriguing because you can keep producing things from them – the children will wonder what's coming next.

- The children will often want to make links between the story and their own experiences. There is no hard and fast rule about when to do this. If you are 'on a roll' with the atmosphere building nicely and your retelling is going with a swing, hold up a warning hand if someone tries to interrupt. Children will come to understand that they will get a turn to say something in a little while. On the other hand, some stories are episodic and you can easily stop for a chat in the middle. When you get to the end of a story, a question which invites links with the children's lives will lead to richer talk than just 'Did you like that story?' which tends to elicit a yes/no answer. It's hard for children at this age to put into words why they liked something, whereas you can get a lengthier response by asking 'Have you ever got separated from your mummy?' (*Owl Babies* again) or ask about whatever befell the characters in the story. Try then to make a link between what a child has said and the text. Moving to and fro between the text and one's own experience is a fundamental 'reading behaviour' which you are helping the children to get started on. Again, you might tell a story about something similar that happened to you, but keep it fairly brief.

- Although critical response to a text is not easy for very young children, you can encourage it by asking them to vote on which part they liked best. Children tend to copy each other at this stage, however, so you might not get much variation! Another idea is to put favourite words from the story on the class word wall. You could have a vote for 'our six favourite words'. It might be possible to talk about some of the features of these words – perhaps their spelling patterns or maybe they sound like what they represent, words such as *splash* and *buzz* and *growl.* Again, developing a fascination with words is a terrific legacy you can offer a child.

- Lastly, there is the possibility of making a book – 'Our Book of the Best Bits in Cinderella' perhaps – or you could be a bit more adventurous and try changing the point of view: 'What the Wolf Said About the Three Little Pigs'. This last example would follow on well from some role play, where you have acted the part of the wolf and explained to the children why you acted as you did. A child could possibly have a go at being the wolf or you could bring in someone else. This technique is called 'hot seating' (I shall have more to say about this in the next chapter). Although book writing might seem to fall outside my remit as the subject of this book is speaking and listening, I'm including it because the planning will involve a lot of talking as you and the children decide what words and pictures should go on each page, how you will fasten the book together and where it will be kept when it's finished. In all these decision-making purposes for talk, it's vitally important to encourage positive collaboration and ways of resolving disagreements and difficulties.

Sharing and discussing non-fiction texts

Much of what I've said about sharing stories is applicable to non-fiction. You should still position yourself and the children carefully so that you can all see the book and each other. It's very likely that the book you are sharing will be connected to a topic the teacher is covering with the whole class, and there may well be artefacts, pictures, maps etc. which you can use to enrich the reading session and, as stated above, help to focus the children's attention. There should also be a lot of new vocabulary which you could add to the word wall.

Reading as a complex set of behaviours

Learning to read these days is seen as a **range** of behaviours from the very start (see *Supporting Reading* in this series, p. 4). By this I mean that we now understand the importance of helping children to tackle a non-fiction text in a different way from reading a story. We tend to start a story at the beginning and continue to the end – reading all of it. Plot and characters are essential elements in story reading. These may sometimes be found in some non-fiction books, especially those written for very young children. 'Faction' – a blend of fiction and non-fiction – is a popular way of introducing a topic.

There is, however, a huge variety of types of non-fiction. Sometimes we start at the beginning and go through to the end, e.g. a biography, perhaps, or a recipe. But we don't start reading the telephone directory at A and continue until we find the number we want. When you are sharing a book with a group, it's important to highlight the distinctive features of that particular kind of text. If you are looking at a recipe together, it's important to draw the children's attention to how it's set out: where it tells you what you will need to make the dish (probably set out as a list) and where it tells you what to do (perhaps these points are numbered). Or you might be looking at a calendar and helping the children to work out how to find their birthdays or those of their friends.

An important aspect of sharing both fiction and non-fiction is the non-verbal part of the text. This might include attractive endpapers that you can dwell on before getting into a story. We tend to take our adult understandings of illustrations for granted, but actually there's a lot to talk about and help the children to interpret. In non-fiction, the non-verbal part might be photographs, aerial views, charts or diagrams – perhaps even a cutaway or cross-section diagram of a castle. You can begin the process of exploring with the children how each of these gives us a different kind of information.

As with the story sharing, you should be able to explore links with the children's own experience and you might be able to help them to create a display – of their teddy bears, maybe, or photographs of themselves or their mums and dads as babies. This offers another opportunity to celebrate cultural diversity in the class. There will be strong links with many aspects of the National Curriculum. Whatever you are doing, try to involve the children in as much of the decision-making as you can. It takes more time and a lot of patience, but it's crucial in making them active learners, which, as I emphasised at the beginning of this chapter, is very important.

Sharing and discussing poems and songs

Some children are taught nursery rhymes at home but many these days are not – or they may come from other cultures and have their own poems and songs. If you can, try to share a range of these. They are enjoyable because they have a strong rhythm or recognisable rhyme scheme, but I often wonder what children make of the meaning of:

> See saw, Margery Daw,
> Johnny shall have a new master.
> He shall have but a penny a day
> Because he can't work any faster.

The obscurity of the meaning, however, doesn't seem to deter them in the least from belting the words out with gusto.

Developing phonological awareness

An important aspect of becoming a reader is recognising rhyming patterns. As a further development, children should be encouraged to invent rhymes of their own. You can help by sharing new versions of old favourites: 'Humpty Dumpty sat on a wall' could be changed to 'Humpty Dumpty went for a walk, met [name of a child] and stopped for a...' (Of course, we are talking about recognising sound patterns here: the children will not be aware of the spellings of 'walk' or 'talk'.)

You can play other games with the children that will help them to develop rhyming strings, such as 'I went to town and I bought a... hat/bat/cat/mat' with each child in turn saying all the words and trying to add a new one. They also need to be encouraged to listen for the individual sounds (phonemes) in words, starting with the initial sound. Old favourites such as 'I spy' are helpful for this, and games like 'The vicar's cat is a(n)... awful, beautiful, creepy, daring etc. ... cat ' with children taking it in turns to come up with the next adjective, keeping to the alphabetical order.

Action rhymes and songs are great fun and also have the merit of encouraging children to string quite a lot of words together without having to think of what to say. They also usually require a variety of emphases, volume, pitch etc. from the speakers. This is helpful for all young children, but particularly for EAL learners.

Play

> Well-planned play is a key way in which children learn with enjoyment and challenge during the Foundation Stage. (DfEE/QCA 2000: 7)

Whole books have been devoted to the importance of play (see some suggested reading at the end of this chapter). Here I can only touch on some of the ways in which you, as a teaching assistant, can help the teacher and the children in this key area of learning.

Planning and resourcing a challenging environment

I have been fortunate enough to be associated with a school which is extremely good at creating wonderful environments for the children to play in, all planned on a two-year rolling programme. The children might arrive one morning to find that in their absence the entire Early Years Unit has been transformed into a healthy food cafe or a farm – or we might be under the sea or in the jungle. Often the environment that has been created is linked to a book the children are sharing and working with, such as *Bob the Builder* or *Elmer*. Any teaching assistant with creative skills – or just a willingness to wield a staple gun – will be very welcome in a school like this.

Using the environment to the best advantage

If the environment is to be anything more than a marvellous visual and tactile experience, the children's learning will need to be supported with some planned play activity. Extra adult input is so enriching here: you might model the making of appointments in a 'hospital' reception area or ask advice about what beauty treatments are available at the 'salon'. Returning to the theme of outside visitors, someone could be invited to show the children how to bandage an arm, which you could then follow up by offering yours for the children to practise on! As I have said before, look for opportunities to encourage co-operation, negotiation and decision-making. Try to ensure that there are opportunities for adult support in a range of the children's languages.

Many children are very literal in their use of language and will need a lot of encouragement in the area of 'Let's pretend'. Don't always provide a crown or a piece of pretend cake or even some coins even though you might be tempted – encourage the children to see the cake in their imaginations and behave as if it was there in reality. Hopefully the children will follow your example.

Nursery rhymes that you have shared with the children can become a focus for some simple drama with you taking either a leading or a supporting role. Little Bo-Peep, for example, played by a child, could be found crying and asked to explain why. You and the children could go on an expedition to find the sheep and on the way you could interview people who might be able to help. You might be able to persuade Humpty Dumpty or even the Grand Old Duke of York to say whether they have seen any sign of the sheep. Caretakers, lunchtime assistants or visitors to the school might be persuaded to say a few words – children from older classes almost certainly will if they happen to be passing.

Help the children to put into words what they are doing or have done. This might be a comment such as 'Oh, I see, you're going to put some rollers in my hair, are you?' Or later, you might encourage them to tell you about how they have spent the time. You can also help them by giving them some vocabulary for what you saw them doing: 'You were mending the car, weren't you, and then Gemma came and asked you to take them to the seaside ... and what did you say then?'

The *Curriculum Guidance for the Foundation Stage* contains a detailed list of the significant opportunities that play offers to children. These include:

- Helping them to make sense of the world.
- Practising and building up ideas, concepts and skills.
- Learning to control impulses.
- Learning to be alone and to be with others.
- Taking risks.
- Thinking creatively and imaginatively.
- Communicating with others in problem-solving.
- Expressing fears and reliving anxious experiences in controlled and safe situations (DfEE/QCA 2000: 25).

Language accompanying action

There are other subjects, such as technology, PE, ICT, science and maths, which will lend themselves to a slightly different kind of talk from that I have discussed so far – talk that accompanies some cutting, weighing, measuring, jumping and lots of other practical activities. Technology calls for designing, making and evaluating; science gives rise to experimenting and testing; maths involves categorising and ordering.

Again modelling is a key task – the children need to know what kinds of questions to ask in these situations. Once what the children are going to make has been decided on, you can ask 'How can we . . . ?' Perhaps improvisation is needed: 'What shall we use for . . . ?' or 'Will it work if . . . ?'

Children have been used to accompanying action with talk since they were very small:

Shall we put your socks on? (Parent does it.)
We'll have a story and then it's bedtime. (Book appears.)

The Russian psychologist, Vygotsky, pointed out that eventually children take over this 'talk accompanying action' to direct themselves. As we get older, the talk appears to fade away, but according to Vygotsky, what really happens is that it becomes silent or 'inner' speech inside our heads. Really, we are telling ourselves what to do next most of the time. What's interesting is that in moments of stress, we find ourselves bringing this 'inner speech' out into the open again: just take note next time you are multitasking even more frenetically than usual.

In school, the activities will become more complex than they were at home and the children should be supported in talking through how they will tackle them. They might be carrying out a test, for example, to find out which material lets water through and which is waterproof, so that they can design a jacket for teddy. What will they do first? Try hard not to over-direct, but to confirm, support and occasionally check if you see a child heading off in a very unproductive direction.

There will be talk associated with using the computer – helping the children to remember how to use the printer, for example.

As well as 'talking their way through an activity', the children can also be shown the kinds of talk that adults use when they are doing these things. Having looked at a recipe, for example, you might decide to go ahead and make some tarts. The talk will start with 'What do we need to do first?' (Wash hands perhaps.) Having looked at what's needed, there's discussion about where to find things – the tin, the ingredients, the tools. What are they all for? What do you do with a sieve? There are special cooking expressions: 'Take' 100 grams of butter, 'rub it in' to the flour, 'roll out the pastry' and make the shapes using a special 'pastry cutter'. But we haven't got one of those, so how can we get round the problem? Later, we exercise great caution getting the hot tin out of the oven. We let the tarts cool – and we share them. 'Are they good?' or 'Would you like another one?' or 'Thank you, they're delicious' are all expressions to try out. Try to keep a special eye out for the EAL speakers and ensure that they are participating fully.

My activities may not be the ones you would choose and you may be surprised that something you have tried and enjoyed doing in class is not here. As I have already said, the possibilities for talk across the curriculum are almost endless and all I have done is to indicate the range of purposes for which you might try to plan. In conclusion, however, could I just remind you again of the range of roles I believe you should adopt. However you put them into practice, these are what I think you should aim for:

- Being a model for the kinds of things that are said and how to say them.
- Encouraging the children to interact confidently with other children and with a range of adults.
- Listening carefully and responding to what the children have to say – putting them in control as much as possible.
- Encouraging children to expand on their comments and answers.

Summary

In this chapter I have looked at:

- A whole-school approach to the development of speaking and listening.
- Supporting children in their speaking and listening as they move into the world of school.
- Ways in which a teaching assistant can help the children to move on as speakers and listeners in accordance with the requirements of the *Curriculum Guidance for the Foundation Stage*.

Further reading

Clipson-Boyles, S. (2001) *Supporting Language and Literacy, 3–8*. London: David Fulton Publishers (esp. Ch. 8).

DfEE/QCA (2000) *Curriculum Guidance for the Foundation Stage*. London: DfEE/QCA

Griffiths, N. (2001) *Storysacks*. Reading: University of Reading, Reading and Language Information Centre.

Mukherji, P. and O'Dea, T. (2000) *Understanding Children's Language and Literacy*. London: Nelson Thornes (esp. Ch. 4).

Tassoni, P. and Hucker, K. (2000) *Planning Play and the Early Years*. London: Heinemann.

Tizard, B. and Hughes, M. (1986) *Young Children Learning: Talking and Thinking at Home and at School*. London: Fontana.

Wells, Gordon (1987) *The Meaning Makers: Children Learning Language and Using Language to Learn*. London: Hodder & Stoughton.

Chapter 5

Talking and learning in Years 1 and 2

Even if you are mainly interested in Key Stage 1, I hope that you will also read through some of the previous chapter on the development of talk in the Foundation Stage. Many of the ideas and activities described there will still be relevant in Years 1 and 2 and many children, though chronologically in Year 1, in development terms may actually still be in the Foundation Stage. They will, however, all be 'old hands' at coming to school, finding their way around, using the equipment and so on.

Extending the opportunities for talk in Key Stage 1

The diagram on p. 43 still applies here. Talk will not come 'out of nothing' but from the exciting and challenging range of situations that the school can provide.

What should you be doing?

The roles listed at the end of Chapter 4 are all just as important in Key Stage 1, but more might be added. I've tried to focus on the specific help that you can give as a teaching assistant. I appreciate that some of the time, you will be doing the same sorts of things as the class teacher is doing with the whole class, but your special contribution must be in your work with groups and individuals. I hope that you will be given opportunities to work in different types of group. DfES/QCA suggests what advantages a **range** of groups might offer:

Characteristics of the talk of boys and girls often differ. Girls are generally more collaborative, supporting each other and developing ideas together. Boys often like to propose ideas, to use language dramatically and to move on fast rather than develop detail. Such differences can be tackled, and children's repertoires extended, by planning different groups, partners, classroom seating and activities. (2003a: 12)

The QCA also advocates grouping according to age (sometimes same age groups, sometimes older with younger), or to first language, number of children, ability or confidence (DfES/QCA 2003a: 21). Using talk partners might be a way of working that you would find useful. Children then have an opportunity to share ideas with someone else, express opinions or carry out some planning. In one school I have worked in children were so used to working with their talk partners that they would consult them spontaneously whenever they felt the need. As I suggested in the last chapter, it's a good idea to vary the talk partners of children who are still learning to speak English so that they get plenty of opportunities to work in both or all their languages.

One of the most valuable things you can do is to provide opportunities for children, individually or in small groups, to consolidate some of the learning they have experienced in the whole-class situation. In the *Speaking, Listening and Learning Handbook* (DfES/QCA 2003a: 17) it states that 'there should be opportunities, both planned and incidental, for children to revisit, apply and extend the speaking and listening skills which they have been explicitly taught'. This is particularly true for children who are still in the early stages of speaking English. I have already enumerated some of the fairly simple talk skills which children should be encountering in the last chapter. In this chapter and the next, I will show you how they get progressively more demanding. In consolidating their oracy skills, it's likely that you will also be revisiting some of the topics across the curriculum that the children are covering. Speaking and listening skills cannot be practised in a vacuum – it is the genuine learning contexts, rather than the contrived activities, which lead to the best results in speaking and listening.

As children move on from the Foundation Stage into tackling the National Curriculum, there will inevitably be more emphasis on subject content or vocabulary associated with the topic, if subjects are grouped together. You can help children to consolidate their grasp of this vocabulary by using it yourself and by giving them as many opportunities as possible to use it in their own discussions. Examples might include:

- What is meant by the concept of a 'fair test' in science.
- Using words such as 'speed' and 'distance' after a lesson on 'forces'.
- When discussing a story, using words such as 'plot' and 'character'.

The DfES/QCA quotes mathematics as an example:

> In number, for example, discussing what happens to a number when multiplied by another number is an opportunity to introduce the vocabulary of multiplication. (2003a: 13)

You might be surprised by the amount of technical vocabulary expected in Key Stage 1 these days. 'Phoneme', 'grapheme' and 'alliteration' are only three of the words that I have heard Year 2 and some Year 1 children using confidently.

Subjects not only have a vocabulary – there are ways of thinking associated with 'being a scientist' or 'thinking like a historian'. And this means that the purposes and types of talk will differ from subject to subject – hypothesising, experimenting, classifying, imagining, describing and predicting are only a few examples.

Another one of your roles is helping the teacher to assess the speaking and listening. Most of these will be informal assessments and should be shared in some form with the children and their parents. An aspect of talk thus becomes more obviously something that they are conscious of working on in the same way as they might work on a particular spelling or a skill in football (for more on this see Chapter 7).

The National Curriculum

From the year in which they reach their fifth birthday, children are legally entitled to receive full coverage of the National Curriculum Programme of Study for Speaking and Listening at Key Stage 1. There should be a clear sense in the school's planning of taking the children on from the early learning goals. In 2003, the DfES/ QCA issued a pack of materials which

I have already referred to: *Speaking, Listening and Learning: Working with Children in Key Stages 1 and 2*. These materials give very clear guidance on how to carry out the National Curriculum requirements for speaking and listening. The teaching objectives and classroom activities in the materials are related to the four aspects of speaking and listening in the National Curriculum:

- Speaking
- Listening
- Group discussion and interaction
- Drama

It would be very useful, if you have not already done so, to obtain these materials and study them closely.

In one booklet in the pack of materials, *Teaching Objectives and Classroom Activities*, you will find four teaching objectives for each term (Year 1 Term 1–Year 6 Term 3), one for each of the areas listed above. Examples of appropriate activities for each objective are also given. These are helpful for schools which are uncertain of their direction as regards the programmes of study for speaking and listening, but they are quite prescriptive. I am sure that most schools after a while will want to devise their own activities.

It is interesting to note how the activities have been distributed across the curriculum. In every term, there is at least one explicit link made between a speaking and listening objective and one in the *National Literacy Strategy Framework for Teaching* (DfEE 1998). Another principle is that at least one objective should be taught in the context of a foundation subject; the remaining two may be contextualised in English, mathematics or other foundation subjects.

In this chapter and the next, I will cover each of the four areas – Speaking, Listening, Group discussion and interaction, Drama – taking my examples from English/drama, mathematics or a foundation subject. I hope that reading these chapters will help to give you the confidence, in collaboration with the classroom teacher, to develop your own activities while remaining within the QCA guidelines. In many cases, you will find that combining two or more areas makes sense: progress in group discussion, for example, will almost inevitably involve some of the speaking and some of the listening objectives but you should tease these out into specific elements for assessment and recording (see Chapter 7).

English

Telling stories, real and imagined, and listening to stories (NC En1, 8a/9b)

Much of what was said about story reading and storytelling in Chapter 4 still applies. There should be an expectation that the children will be able to sit and listen with more sustained concentration, though this may not always be the case.

What other signs of progress might you look for?

By this time, children are more experienced 'consumers' as far as stories are concerned. They should have heard enough of them to have some idea of how stories shape up. There are, according to Pie Corbett (2001), about eight basic 'story shapes' including the losing tale, the tale of a quest and the tale of defeating the monster (for more on this see *Supporting Reading* in this series, p. 31).

It's a good idea to encourage children to think about the shape of the story they are listening to – you can do this by stopping at key moments and asking the group to tell you what they think will happen next. Probe a little bit about the reasons behind the children's answers. Are they in fact drawing on their knowledge of other books like this one or are they using their own experiences and 'knowledge of the world?' Encourage them to use both of those to answer your question having thought very carefully about how the story has gone so far.

In deciding what might happen next, encourage the children to interpret the pictures as well as the text. This will be particularly helpful for EAL children. Because you are doing the reading, or the telling, the stories can be more complex than if the children were to tackle them alone. Exploit this situation to get the struggling readers hooked on a really enjoyable story, with beautiful illustrations, to counteract the difficulties some of them may be having with reading independently.

You might like to ask the children to suggest an alternative ending or a slightly different version. For example, what if, when Prince Charming arrives at Cinderella's house, the glass slipper fits one of the ugly sisters? What would happen next?

You could make a map or diagram or find a picture related to the book you are sharing and ask children to fix labels to appropriate parts: 'This is where Snow White was left in the woods.' 'This is the house of the seven dwarfs.' 'This is the path they go down when they go to work.' This also motivates children who are still finding decoding difficult as well as the second language learners – they will want to join in the reading and placing of the labels.

If you have the opportunity to start a new book with a group, you could conceal part of the book cover with sheets of paper and Blu-Tack. Ask the children to predict what they think the book will be about. Peel the paper back bit by bit if necessary (or show them the picture on the cover, but not the title). You will probably be aware that much more attention is paid nowadays in the teaching of reading to the book as an object. Children in Key Stage 1 are expected to understand and use terms such as 'author', 'illustrator', 'title' and 'publisher'. They may discuss the fact that the book is dedicated to someone or that it has an ISBN number (see *Supporting Reading* in this series, p. 64).

Children are also introduced to a wide range of genres or types of book – whether in their reading scheme or in the non-scheme books that are shared with them. It's important for them to learn to find clues about what to expect from a particular book. Is it likely to be fiction or non-fiction? If fiction, do they recognise the name of the author? What is the story likely to be about? The cover will give some clues and you will also probably want to share the blurb on the back of the book, if there is one.

You may well find yourself helping children in Year 1 or Year 2 to consult non-fiction texts to find the answer to a question they have asked themselves. Here too you need to guide them in how to decide whether a particular book is likely to have the information they're looking for. If it does look suitable, how do they locate the correct pages or sections? Discourage flicking through the book from cover to cover, and support the use of chapter or page headings, indexes and so on. It's most important that children at this stage come to realise that reading is a set of behaviours: telephone directories, recipes, poems, stories and even their own work when they are proof-reading it – all these count as 'reading' but all are tackled in different ways (for more on this see *Supporting Reading* in this series, p. 4).

Not only do children have a wider knowledge of story form at this age, they also have some knowledge of the structure of sentences. In other words, many of them are quite expert in the grammar of their language. This does not mean that they can tell you which word is a preposition or a conjunction, nor can they distinguish between a simple and a complex sentence, but they use all of these, all the time. Their knowledge is implicit, not explicit.

To help them to develop their awareness of sentence patterns, once you have started reading, you could leave out certain words and ask the children to try to identify the missing words. Praise the children if their suggestions make sense and are appropriate in the context, even if they are not the actual words used by the writer. As well as developing sentence knowledge and vocabulary, you are also encouraging a sense of style. Do we really want to describe the wolf in *Little Red Riding Hood* as 'bad' or are there more exciting words? How about 'terrifying' or 'ferocious'? Again, it doesn't matter if no one can spell these words. They will enjoy saying them – though you could put them up for interest on the word wall so that the children can see what they look like. Encourage the children to have fun with the words. The day after reading *Little Red Riding Hood* you could start another story session by asking 'What was the wolf like?' and let everyone shout out 'He was ferocious' as loud as they can. Try to get all the children to join in, even if the word is a very difficult one for some of them. You could help by pointing out the initial sound and comparing it with the first sound in someone's name.

Punctuation is something else to draw the children's attention to at this stage. You could make them aware of punctuation marks by talking about what you did with your voice as you asked a question, or showed alarm or surprise. What marks in the text show us how to read it? You could talk about speech in a similar way. How do we know the words that come out of people's mouths? How do we know how to say them? Let the children stand up and point to the marks on the page (you could make a pointing stick with a hand on the end of it).

You will probably find that in Year 1 and Year 2 there are more children who are prepared to have a go at 'hot seating' (described on p. 70) but instead of going into role yourself, ask one of the children to take it on and let the others interview them. You could allow the class to work with talk partners to come up with some questions.

As well as listening to you telling or reading a story, a story tape could be shared with a group. You can use a commercial tape, one that you have asked someone to record, or perhaps one that the children or some older children have recorded. One advantage of this is that you can incorporate a range of accents into the story readings – even if you are not very good at them yourself. You can also enable the children to hear male voices reading stories (apologies if you are a male – most of the teaching assistants I have come across have been female!). Many children seem to grow up believing that the reading and telling of stories is a female preserve – perhaps not suitable for boys – and we need to disabuse them of this idea as early as possible.

Freed from the responsibility of presenting the story yourself, you can watch the children's reactions closely and see who is finding it hard to maintain concentration.

When you have listened to a story with the children, encourage them to discuss what features they think made the storytelling effective. A good use of accents might be one criterion, but they should be able to come up with others. You could help the group to put together a poster for the classroom wall listing all the criteria which they can then refer to in their own storytelling.

Reading aloud, as the DfES/QCA (2003a) makes clear, helps children to become familiar with the cadences and uses of English. If children *are* to be asked to read aloud, I prefer to give them an opportunity to prepare the passage first, whether it's a 'live' reading, in assembly perhaps, or on tape, as suggested here. I can then insist on the 'speaking clearly, fluently and confidently' which is the first item in the Key Stage 1 Programme of Study for Speaking and Listening. Many older and much more experienced readers hate being asked to read aloud without warning, and I think that children should get used to the idea of this aspect of reading as a 'performance' which needs some preparation. The old habit of bringing out 'the book you are on' and reading a page to the teacher has disappeared from many schools, thanks to the literacy hour in which shared and guided reading have become the norm (see *Supporting Reading* in this series). Personally, I think its passing is a good thing – many of my students have said that they remembered it as a fearful time, with everyone in the class waiting for you to slip up and make a fool of yourself. If this practice is still carried out, at least children should be given the opportunity to read over and prepare the page silently before reading it aloud. If the book is new to the child, I would read through it – all of it – first, with the child listening, so that they get the hang of how it goes, rather than plodding through it a page at a time in a blinkered fashion.

Last but by no means least, provide plenty of opportunities for children to tell stories themselves. It's difficult to stop some of them, but others may only join in with a little encouragement. Their stories will often be about things that have happened to them, as in the old 'news' sessions, but look out for and encourage more 'bookish' storytelling, where children use the vocabulary and structures they have heard you use as you read to them. Try a storytelling circle: you can either go round from person to person or start the story yourself and then stop from time to time, pointing to someone who must then take over. If you are working with second language learners, keep the sentences quite clearly structured with lots of repetition.

Drama

Working in role, presenting drama to others, responding to performances (NC En1, 11a, b, c)

If you have not worked in schools for very long, it's possible that your sole experience of drama in an educational setting has been attending the Christmas play. You may feel rather apprehensive about teaching it, perhaps seeing it as an art form which requires specialist knowledge: a subject in its own right. You might feel that it is more akin to movement, music and dance than to language development. On the other hand, you may see it as a way of increasing children's oral confidence. Does it develop collaborative and social skills or is it rather a process of self-exploration? Is it an end in itself or a means of learning across the curriculum? In fact, taken as a whole, drama can encompass all these opportunities. There is no need to polarise them.

What are the advantages of teaching drama, and through drama?

- Drama is a fundamental part of all human culture. 'Putting on an act' is something we all do instinctively, and something we respond eagerly to, especially when it's done by skilled performers.
- Drama is appealing and motivating to children.
- Like art, music, dance or gymnastics it offers children opportunities to be creative.
- It's an efficient way of teaching because drama as a teaching tool enables children to be active learners and meaning-makers. They can take what they have been told, or have read, and make it part of their own point of view. Usually, this act of putting information to some use leads to a willingness to spend longer on a task and to more effective retention of learning.

You will see, I hope, from the above, that I am arguing the case for integrating drama with other learning objectives in science, maths and history – almost any area of the curriculum. But we do also need to look at drama as a subject in its own right with its own specialist skills and vocabulary. This includes helping children to evaluate dramatic performances they have seen, just as much as books they have read. This is quite a tall order at Key Stage 1, but this aspect can be started there and continued in Key Stage 2. Year 1 and Year 2 children may not possess many of the specialist vocabulary skills of drama, but they can talk about a live or recorded performance they have seen, and say what they enjoyed in their own words. The journey home in the coach from a live performance is an ideal time to encourage this 'reviewing' kind of talk as the out-of-school setting encourages children to speak up and say what they think.

The box summarises the range of activities that drama can encompass:

| Drama as a means of increasing oral confidence and fluency. | Drama as a way of exploring ideas and feelings – often starting from literature but making links with personal experience. | Drama as a set of performance skills. |

You can, of course, be doing some or all of these at the same time, though the chances are that only one will be emphasised, especially if you are assessing the activity.

What activities to choose?

If it's taught badly, drama can be a woolly business – at its worst ending up with a heap of 'baddies' fighting about you can't imagine what in the middle of the classroom. But turn your mind away from that thought – that's the result of poor planning. Together with the class teacher, you need to clarify your learning objectives before you take your group off to find a place to work.

What do you want the children to learn?

What experiences will you provide to support the learning?

What's the focus? What information will they be using?
How much time will it take?

How will you consolidate their understanding?
What will *you* be doing? How will you assess?

Working in role

Learning objectives

In general terms, the objectives of role-play work are:

- Increasing understanding of the experiences and feelings of your character.
- Exploring an unfamiliar context.
- Responding to events and dealing with relationships. Some of these are familiar, such as family events and relationships; others are very unfamiliar, involving monsters, dragons or princesses etc.

● Making decisions (something children don't usually get very much chance to do).

Techniques

At Key Stage 1 you will just be introducing children to these – they can be developed and added to at Key Stage 2.

Hot seating

This has been mentioned several times already. It's a good technique for focusing closely on a character and getting at the motivation for their actions. It also enables you to explore the gaps in a character's story. You might, for example, ask a child to pretend to be Little Bear in *Let's Go Home, Little Bear* by Martin Waddell. Little Bear has had a pretty frightening time in the forest (though really, there was no need to be afraid because Big Bear was always there). He could be asked to describe what the forest was like, and what he thought he heard and saw that made him feel so frightened.

Freeze frames

Freeze frames are still images or silent tableaux which you can use to illustrate a specific incident or event. The children should be asked to think carefully about the positions they take up and what messages they are sending with their bodies. You could set up a tableau of Little Miss Muffet and her friends having a tea party. They haven't seen the spider and are chatting and eating happily. Then show what happens after the spider puts in an appearance – but still in a freeze frame, no running! If you did this with Year 2, they might think the nursery rhyme was rather beneath them, but then you could explain that it was a way to start thinking about *Spider Watching* by Vivian French. This is a text which explores with children whether we really need to be afraid of spiders.

Conscience alley

Conscience alley is a technique for exploring a character's mind at a moment of crisis. It might sound rather sophisticated for Year 1 and indeed it's a technique that can be used very successfully at Key Stage 2 to explore the complexity of the decisions a character is facing. It can, however, also be done at a simpler level. For example, you might have been sharing *Where the Wild Things Are* by Maurice Sendak. As stated above, drama can sometimes be akin to movement or dance and here you might have been allowing the children to explore 'the wild rumpus' that Max enjoys when he's king of the wild things. But suddenly you freeze the action and ask the children to think about what happens next in the story. Then they form two lines. One child must be Max and walk down the 'conscience alley' while the children call out suggestions to him to help him decide what to do. (Some should be urging him to go home because his family miss him and his supper is ready, and others should be urging him to stay and have fun.) In the story, Max decides to go home but your Max might not, which would lead to more interesting discussion about what would happen then.

Dynamic duos

This is one of the simplest and least threatening forms of role play to set up. At a given signal, pairs of children go into role – they may be given the roles or agree them for themselves. They make up the conversation as they go along. Just to give you an illustration from texts we all know, you might ask a child to phone Jack and Jill's mother to find out how they are, or someone might visit Humpty Dumpty in hospital. Stories or poems that you are sharing with Year 1 and Year 2 will almost certainly give you characters and situations to start from. I prefer to explore around the themes and ideas in a story rather than to use the dialogue in the text itself and 'act it out' – although, of course, both are possible. I certainly would not encourage the children to write out a script when doing role-play activities – the whole point here is that they should be improvised.

Sharing the work

Most of what I have discussed here involves improvisation – children making up the dialogue as they go along. Although as I said above, I would not prepare scripts or rehearse any of the above list of activities, some of the freeze frames perhaps, or the pair work, might be interesting to share with the whole class – not as a performance but just on the basis of 'come and see what we've been doing'. Then there may be opportunities for everyone – participants and spectators alike – to discuss what was done, out of role.

Just occasionally, something done in these contexts might be expanded into a more rehearsed performance which could be shared with the whole school in assembly (but the improvisation then becomes something else).

This is too big a topic to cover fully in this book, but you can find more ideas in the QCA materials mentioned above and in the books listed at the end of the chapter. Just before I leave the topic, however, I would like to offer a few helpful hints!

- Restrict the amount of time you allow for these activities, especially at Key Stage 1 – two or three minutes is often long enough before things start to go off the boil.

- Show that you value the activities – this can often come from taking part in them yourself. This also gives you the opportunity to model language of different kinds, to use or introduce new words and to find out what the children are thinking or what they remember.

- Try to put the child in the role of expert. Avoid taking over.

- Use an agreed signal, such as a whistle or a drum, when you want the children to freeze. Be consistent with this and insist on an immediate response.

Drama as performance (NC En1, 11c: presenting drama and stories to others)

While role play requires children to think and talk their way into a situation, formulating meaning as they go along, to plan and rehearse a performance enables them to work on shaping the words (if they are their own or other children's) or to learn and present someone else's words.

You might, for example, take your group to another class to share a story you have acted out, using children in role or with puppets. This gives you a good opportunity to discuss with your group whether some aspects of the performance need any clarification: 'Do you think they'll understand the bit where...?'

A Reception/Year 1 class shared a reading of the poem 'Big Bare Bear' (Foster 1993). The children discussed the poem's story and the characters. One response, after looking at the pictures, was 'That hairy bear is not nice. He's all pointy.' The teacher encouraged the child to expand on her idea:

What do you mean by not nice? What did he do to make you think that?

He popped the nice bear's balloon and made him fall.

The children dramatised the poem as a whole class, talking a lot about the 'plot' and 'characters'. Then it was set to music and they performed it in assembly. The teaching assistant's role was to help a small group to portray their characters by asking questions such as 'How could we let the audience know you're nasty?'

The most sophisticated aspect of performance drama is the school play. This is a time-consuming business and many schools feel that they can no longer fit it into a crowded timetable. It certainly provides opportunities for children to speak at length. Freed from the burden of thinking what to say, they can be encouraged to pay attention to saying the lines in a way appropriate for their character. There is good motivation to speak clearly and loudly.

One of the areas in which we should be looking for some progress in Key Stage 1 is in the ability to listen with sustained concentration. This doesn't come easily. I was enjoying a performance of a nativity play last Christmas where the difficulties were made abundantly clear. It wasn't just a question of keeping the crowds of angels, shepherds etc. focused throughout – even Mary's mind had clearly drifted off, and she was picking her nose at the crucial moment when Gabriel told her she was going to have a baby.

How could you encourage more sustained listening?

You will find some useful suggestions in another publication by the DfEE/QCA (1999), one of which is to invite the school meals provider to visit the classroom and tell the children what is on the menu for lunch, describing five items. Explain that the class is going to play a memory game and ask the visitor to remind them of the five items before leaving. The children can be told to create pictures in their minds to help them to remember the items. Before lunch, working with talk partners, ask one child to name the items and the other to check and agree. Discuss the method of remembering with the whole class.

Mathematics

Some National Curriculum requirements:

- Use the correct language, symbols and vocabulary associated with number and data (Ma2e).
- Communicate in spoken, pictorial and written form, at first using informal language and recording, then mathematical language and symbols (Ma2f).
- Understand a general statement and investigate whether particular cases match it (Ma2h).
- Explain their methods and reasoning when solving problems involving number and data (Ma2i).

There should be plenty of opportunities for you to follow up work the teacher has carried out with the whole class, but here are some ideas.

Sequencing

You might give the children a series of numbers or shapes and ask them to tell you not only what comes next but also their criteria for their answer. For example:

| 2 | 4 | 8 | 16 |

Ask the children to describe how the patterns in the second example are building. Can they make the next one from matchsticks? Can they make the tenth pattern? Ask them to tell you how they know.

Giving numbers a context

- I've got three bags full. What could I be thinking of? (Wool – Baa Baa Black Sheep.)
- What if I give one bag away? What if I buy another sheep?
- I've got four and I've got twenty. What could I be thinking of? (Blackbirds baked in a pie.) What if three flew away?

Ask the children to think up some 'what if' questions of their own.

Putting mathematics into a story

- How old do you think Snow White is?
- Is she bigger than you?
- How big are the dwarfs?
- What time do you think the dwarfs go to work?
- How long are they away from home?
- How many breakfast plates does Snow White wash up if everyone has one?

Just reading mathematics aloud to the children with them following is helpful as it will reinforce the meaning of mathematical symbols.

Do a jigsaw with a group but turn all the pieces to the wrong side so that the children have to match them by shape alone. Of course, you need to encourage lots of discussion while you are doing the activity!

▨ Science

By working with children in pairs and small groups you can build on the teacher's work in such activities as:

- Using and extending scientific vocabulary.
- Developing observational skills and describing and explaining what happened.
- Collecting evidence, perhaps by weighing and measuring.
- Talking about what might happen before deciding what to do.
- Comparing what happened with what the children thought might happen.

Here are a few ideas for following up the lesson by the teacher.

- Your group could bring to school photographs of themselves as babies. You could all make a display or help the children to scan the pictures into the computer. The children can compare:

- The time of day/date/season when they were born.
- How much each child weighed.
- How long it was before they got their first tooth or when they lost a tooth.

● You might have the opportunity to take groups of children into the school garden and to help them to choose plants and seeds. You can discuss with them how they will keep records of what was put where/what flourished (and what didn't)/ how much water each plant had/ how long it took each plant to grow.

● The teaching topic might be healthy and unhealthy diets. With your support, the children might carry out a survey of what everyone likes best in their packed lunch. Which of the foods will give them energy? Which will make them put on weight? Which are needed for growth? You can help the children to design and produce a simple questionnaire and a way of recording their findings. This kind of work can be very supportive for EAL learners. The sentences should be kept clear and simple, providing the children with a structured opportunity to interact with a range of people.

When you have all the results from a survey such as this, you can generate a lot of talk using the data gathered. Maths will come into the equation too as the children count how many people like apples in their lunch boxes and compare that figure with how many people like crisps, for example.

Summary

In this chapter I have looked at:

● The role of the teaching assistant in extending children's talk throughout Key Stage 1.
● The DfES/QCA materials.
● Opportunities for extending speaking and learning in
  - English
  - Drama
  - Mathematics
  - Science

Further reading

Corbett, P. (2001) *How to Teach Fiction Writing at Key Stage 2.* London: David Fulton Publishers.

DfEE (1998) *National Literacy Strategy Framework for Teaching.* London: DfEE.

DfEE/QCA (1999) *Teaching Speaking and Listening at Key Stage 1 and 2.* London: DfEE/QCA.

DfES/QCA (2003a) *Speaking, Listening and Learning: Working with Children in Key Stages 1 and 2. Handbook.* London: DfES/QCA.

DfES/QCA (2003b) *Speaking, Listening and Learning: Working with Children in Key Stages 1 and 2. Teaching Objectives and Classroom Activities.* London: DfES/QCA.

Foster, John (1993) *Twinkle, Twinkle, Chocolate Bar: Rhymes for the Very Young.* Oxford: Oxford University Press.

Phillips, Sarah (2003) *Drama with Children* (Resource Books for Teachers series). Oxford: Oxford University Press.

Chapter 6

Talking and learning, 8–11 years

I must emphasise again that a child's chronological age is only a rough guide to his/her level of achievement. Even if you are working in Key Stage 2, you will find children who still need a lot of encouragement to speak at some length, to listen for moderate amounts of time and to play an active part in group work and drama of all kinds. The naturally quiet child needs sensitive handling – you will not improve the situation by suggesting that this child should be the one who reads out their work in assembly. They would probably have a sleepless night and not be able to come to school next day! Many adults are naturally quiet. We should try to develop each child's potential, realising that this may take more years than just those spent in primary school, and a lot more experience of life. Here are some ideas you might try.

■ Encouraging the reluctant talker in Key Stage 2

- Don't equate silence with lack of interest or involvement. Praise the child who has obviously been listening quietly and taking everything in.
- Look for occasions when the child will be highly motivated to ask a question or make a comment – perhaps because of a special interest in the topic. But be careful about putting the child on the spot.
- Have a quiet word with the child if you notice him/her taking a more than usually active part in a discussion. Make it clear how pleased you are.
- Give the child errands or jobs to do which will be within his/her range of achievement with a little effort. An example might be to take a

message to the school office. Speak to the secretary beforehand so that s/he can be ready to offer praise and encouragement.

- Put the child in the role of expert whenever you can. Perhaps a new pupil has joined the class and needs to be shown where everything is.

- Try to engage the quiet child in conversation whenever an opportunity arises at breaktime, in the lunch hour or on an out-of-school trip. Start these conversations with a comment of your own rather than a direct question, though obviously you are trying to create an opportunity for the child to join in the conversation.

- Respect the child's home culture and traditions. Many Muslim girls are expected to play a fairly passive role at home. Some children are brought up to be quiet and respectful when with older people, perhaps not even looking at them directly. As the DfES/QCA points out:

> Cultural differences influence the ways children speak to their peers and adults. Children need carefully organised opportunities to learn different ways of interacting and to work with others who are more confident and versatile. (2003a: 12)

Is your role different from that of the Key Stage 1 teaching assistant?

This is more a question of emphasis than a change of role. You will still be an important model for a range of kinds of talk, but by this time you may feel that you are putting more of your efforts into encouraging successful pupil interaction (and pupil/adult interaction). Some of the tasks set by the teacher may well have a speaking and listening outcome. Examples might include:

- A prepared talk.
- A report.
- A performance.
- A rehearsed reading.

Your support will be important in all of this, especially at the lower end of Key Stage 2. These are more formal kinds of talk, more remote from the children's everyday experience, and your advice and suggestions as a 'friendly critical listener' during the preparation time will be invaluable (for more on 'formal' talk, see below).

It's also vital that you validate talk by making clear how important it is. One way of doing this is to help the children to see what they have achieved. There's still a tendency for some children to feel that talking is for infants and that writing is their most important task. You might hear them say 'We didn't do any work today, we just talked.' There are various ways in which you can help them to review and realise their achievements:

- By providing opportunities to talk over the work that has been done, with their talk partners.
- By asking children to keep a talk log (see Chapter 7).
- By occasionally taping a discussion so that you can highlight good points – and perhaps points for development – later.
- By teaching the children the appropriate terminology for discussing talk (see below).
- By using children as observers of others' talk and asking them to comment on what they thought were the highlights of a discussion.

Giving the children opportunities to talk about talk

You will see from the bullet points above that I now have an additional focus to those in Key Stage 1. In each of those bullet points, except the first one, I'm not just talking about 'learning through talk' but also about helping the children to reflect on the actual process of discussion and the part they played in it. This can happen to some extent in Key Stage 1, but by the time they reach Key Stage 2 most children can go much further.

How do you support children in reflecting on and improving their talk skills?

Part of your role now is to help the teacher to provide opportunities for 'reflective moments' in small groups. You can help the children to identify those aspects of talking together that help – or hinder – a successful outcome, where everyone feels satisfied with the part they have played. If you 'talk about talk' you might need a language for discussing it, sometimes referred to as a 'metalanguage'. So long as it's not overdone, children enjoy using technical terms – it helps to build up a feeling of shared expertise as well as defining some concepts more precisely.

Some of the aspects of talk that you will want to discuss in these reflective moments with a group of children are dealt with below. From time to time, a few examples of metalanguage will be introduced but you should not feel obliged to introduce technical terms – they are only useful if they genuinely help to pin down a concept or to clarify your/the children's thinking.

Speaking

Children will be expected to speak at greater length. Sometimes this might happen spontaneously but most of us would expect to make some notes if we were 'making a speech'. The concept of 'the long turn' should be familiar to the children. If children do speak at length, their listeners will switch off unless they speak clearly and hold their listeners' attention in some way. Gestures might play an important part as will eye contact. Sometimes the children may be using a visual aid. If so, it's important to help them to think about how to make it visible, not to wave it about and – perhaps most importantly – to ensure that the audience is not too distracted by it so that they stop listening. As they reflect on how successful they were, children should be able to incorporate some or all of these points into making their judgements.

Formal language

This is a sensitive and quite a complex subject! You may find it helpful to look again at Chapter 2 where these issues are discussed at some length (pp. 14–25). Having read that chapter, you should feel clear about the contrasts in ways of speaking illustrated below:

Formal ————————————————————informal

Standard ————————————————————non-standard

Depending on where your school is situated, you may or may not come across many examples of non-standard English in the pupils' speech. You will remember from Chapter 2 that the term 'non-standard' refers to examples of regional vocabulary and grammar and not to accent. The DfES/QCA (2003a: 23), in line with the National Curriculum, is keen that all children can and should use standard English: 'Progression in speaking and listening is related to children's ability to use standard English appropriately.'

Learning to use 'formal' English, on the other hand, applies to every child, whether from the regions or the home counties. The concepts of 'purpose', 'audience' and 'setting' (introduced in Chapter 1) are very relevant here. Formal language is most frequently used where the speakers do not have a close relationship: 'Progression in speaking and listening is related to children's ability to adapt to different circumstances and contexts with independence and confidence (DfES/QCA 2003a: 23).

Drama is one of the ways to open up discussions on all these aspects of language use – both the drama the children themselves are involved in and evaluations of performances live or on screen. I will have more to say about how it might help, later in this chapter.

Listening

- Draw the children's attention to what the DfES/QCA (2003a) refers to as 'listening and responding strategies'. An attentive listener follows up the points made by a speaker, confirming some points and politely disagreeing with others.

- A keen listener might politely ask for more information.

- A critical listener is able to identify some of the presentational features speakers use to put their points across effectively.

- A discriminating listener is well aware of the differences between formal and informal language, knows how to make the right choices and recognises when others have done so.

- An alert listener recognises when s/he is being 'got at' even in the nicest possible way, i.e. when strategies are being used as a means of persuasion. This is a useful skill in today's world when all sorts of speakers are vying with each other to persuade us to be/do/buy/believe etc.

● A skilful listener can listen to a substantial amount of information, perhaps from a variety of sources on a film or video and make relevant notes.

Group discussion

By the time the children reach Key Stage 2, the group discussion might be speculative or it might be expected to lead to action of some kind. There should be clear structures and deadlines to which children should learn to adhere. Maintaining the momentum in the group can be extremely difficult and, while not taking the group over, you could nevertheless help to ensure that things move along at a reasonable pace. If the group grinds to a halt, you can be instrumental in helping the children to reflect on what went wrong.

It's likely that there will be roles to be allocated which, perhaps, the children will decide for themselves – again you could offer support. Tasks and resources may need to be shared out. The role of chairperson is a vital one, and when the task is completed you can help the children to think about what makes an effective chair. Were all the participants encouraged to have their say? Did the chairperson sum up effectively at any point? Other children might be sent as 'emissaries' to another group and then report back their findings to their home group (for more on ways of using groups like this see p. 92).

Sometimes children assume roles rather than having them officially allocated. Some are good at playing the role of 'teacher', bringing the group back on task if they have strayed into something irrelevant. Others are good at opening up the discussion again if it has come to too hasty a conclusion. You can play a vital part in noting these contributions and bringing them to the group's attention later. Make sure children receive due praise for their achievements as group facilitators.

One of the crucial things you should note about a group, so that you can give them feedback later, is how they handle disagreements and differences of viewpoint. How well do children accept criticism or a challenge to their cherished opinions? Were the points tactfully made? How did the group decide to move forward? It might be that someone suggested holding a vote. Was that appropriate? Could you genuinely praise any of the children for being prepared to modify or change their points of view? You may have to find ways of bringing up issues of over-dominance – or think of a task or situation which will help the over-dominant children to modify their behaviour.

Perhaps some of the above sounds a bit abstract – even a bit daunting. The points are important because I believe very strongly that we need to be much clearer in schools (than perhaps we have been in the past) about how to take children on in speaking and listening. We need a definite idea of what progress looks like. Sometimes, perhaps, we have been so pleased just to see role play or discussion taking place at all that we have not stopped to ask whether the children in Year 6 are better at these than the children in Year 3 – and how we might know. This, of course, has implications for the assessment of speaking and listening (I shall look more closely at the issues raised in Chapter 7). For now, however, you might find it helpful if I illustrate from a selection of subjects, taught either individually or in topics/themes, so that you can 'put some flesh on the bones' of the points outlined above.

Drama

In this section, I will discuss drama as a subject in its own right, but later I hope to show you how useful and interesting it can be as a learning tool in many curriculum areas at Key Stage 2.

Drama as a subject

Role play

If the teacher you work with is interested in using drama techniques, you may find yourself helping out with, and perhaps even taking part in, an extended role play that may be developed over several weeks. Children should be able to sustain and develop roles over this period of time, linking their work with reading and writing, and perhaps also with theatre visits and other out-of-school activities.

As an example, I will discuss how work could be based on a World War II theme with a Year 6 class. This could be loosely linked with the class or individual reading of one or more novels about the war, such as *Carrie's War* by Nina Bawden or *Goodnight Mr Tom* by Michelle Magorian. The kind of work I have in mind, however, is not specifically using the situations or characters in the novels. Neither is it directly a way of teaching facts about the war. Rather, it is centred on personal relationships and issues which families have to deal with because they happen to be in a war setting. It is up to the teacher to decide how much information and documentation about the war is to be included – perhaps some photographs or artefacts such as ration books (or copies) might be used during the role play, or sound effects such as an air raid siren or the sound of bombing. It's quite possible that the teacher intends to use the interest generated by taking part in the drama as a way into some history teaching, rather than the other way round.

Setting up a learning contract

I have described how children at this stage are required to be more reflective and aware of the methods of learning they are using. As an example, before beginning what is to be a five-week period of drama teaching for perhaps an hour a week, it's important for the teacher to agree a learning contract with the children. They must agree to 'suspend their disbelief', to be willing to behave as if they are a family living in 1939 in the middle of a city that might come under attack. This is vital if the work is to succeed. Also, everyone must be willing to help to build the imaginary world that the teacher opens up. If, for some reason or other, a child is finding that difficult on a particular occasion, s/he should sit out, but avoid putting the efforts of the rest of the group at risk. You may find it difficult to accept, if you have not done this kind of work before, but if the contract works well, it really is possible to forget that you are in the school hall on a Monday morning and that the heating system has not been on for long enough. Of course, a great deal depends on the enthusiasm and dedication of the teacher. I would not recommend that you try to do work like this on your own with a group if it's something the children are not used to in your school.

Getting started

It will be up to the teacher to get the work underway – perhaps by asking the children to form 'photographs' or tableaux in groups, as families or workmates. It's very important to build the children's belief in these roles in the early stages and to have another adult – the teaching assistant – to help is extremely useful. Your job is to go round the room asking the families questions about themselves – what they do for a living, how the war has affected them so far, what kinds of things they do in the evenings and so on. It's a good idea to give yourself a role, perhaps as a journalist or radio reporter. Don't worry if there's lots of giggling at this stage, but don't step out of your role to reprimand the children unless absolutely necessary. It's also not a good idea to correct any anachronisms that crop up while you're doing this. If children say that they watch television in the evening, make a mental note and use it as a discussion point when you are talking over the work with them later. Teachers are used to making evaluative comments when a child says something, such as 'Oh, what a good idea, Janice' or 'Don't be silly, Samantha.' This too is entirely inappropriate here, although you can remember to tell a child afterwards that you thought their ideas were excellent or needed more thinking through. Of course, it's also important for you to encourage the group to reflect on each other's work and contributions in a positive and helpful way.

The teacher will probably suggest other ways in which you can support the drama. Sometimes children are asked to take time out from the role play to draw an outline figure of themselves (as they are in the role play) and to make notes about who they are, what they do, what they look like and so on. They might benefit from some prompting about things you have heard them say or do. These notes will help them to get back into their roles in Week 2 and may also form the basis for some more extended writing such as an autobiography.

Reflecting on the success of the work

If you are asked by the teacher to talk over the work with a group, do this somewhere else if you can: in the classroom if the work has been done in the hall, or in a shared area or reading corner. The changed setting reflects that the drama roles are suspended and that a more evaluative kind of talk is needed.

There are a number of aspects you need to touch on in such an evaluation session:

● Was the group able to deal with the complexity of the issues involved? Of course, we are only talking about Week 1 here, but as the weeks go on, there should be increasing signs of the children taking on board the dangers of living in a city that might be bombed.

- Did the children work well together as a group? Did they all get a chance to contribute ideas? Did they listen to each other's ideas? If there were arguments, did they find successful ways of sorting them out?

- Did the children make good use of the specific drama techniques the teacher suggested? So far, I have referred to making 'photographs' or tableaux and to making 'character posters'. Can the children see ways in which these techniques enabled them to build their belief in their characters?

- Do the children show an ability to use their growing knowledge of speaking, listening and discussion techniques in their evaluations of their own and others' performances?

This is the time to bring up the anachronisms I mentioned earlier – not to make the children feel they were 'wrong', which is not in the spirit of drama teaching, but as a way of helping them to empathise more with the character they are playing. You might need to point out, for example, that there would have been no such thing as a supermarket and that food in any case was scarce. It is important that they think through the consequences of this for their 'family' and decide how to incorporate the new ideas into their role play.

There is not space here to guide you through all aspects of the five week's work. Other techniques already mentioned in the last chapter are likely to be used by the teacher. In Week 2, s/he may introduce the idea of dialogue. As the families sit round the dinner table (without very much food on it!), what are they likely to talk about? Before Session 2, the teacher may put up a poster inviting them all to a meeting to discuss the evacuation of the children. This issue is likely to be the central idea of the next four weeks. Should the children go or stay? Conscience alley techniques and hot seating can be used here (see pp. 70–1).

In those weeks when the children have been encouraged to talk in role, you have an ideal opportunity in your evaluation sessions to discuss the appropriateness of the words chosen, taking into account the characters involved and their situation. It's not only the words that matter, of course, but also how successful the children were in conveying feelings and states of mind. If there was any persuading to be done, or ordering or cajoling, were the appropriate gestures, tones, emphases etc. used? Did a character speak with enough formality – or informality? Should s/he have used standard English, perhaps, or more colloquial English or more regional dialect?

One way in which you might help as the situation develops would be to take on a role such as an Evacuation Officer. You could attend a meeting in the 'town hall' where you try to persuade any reluctant parents to send their children to the countryside, away from danger. Towards the end of the five weeks, you might be asked to meet the evacuees and try to find homes for them or take them into your own home. Or you might be the person writing out name tags at the station and tying them on.

Of course, it is possible for a teacher to use this method of teaching without any extra adult help, but it is very useful to have someone else to join in and more fun for you – even if you feel a bit apprehensive at first!

Performance

If a piece of drama is to be performed then it's likely that some 'theatre skills' will be introduced to the children. These might include:

- Creating visual images by moving in appropriate ways – stately processions/bustling crowds/threatening movements.
- Using stillness and pauses for dramatic effect.
- Slowing speech down and speaking emphatically at times.
- Using physical gestures – perhaps incorporating a prop of some kind such as a sword or a wand.
- Showing relationships to others by physical actions as well as speech.

No teaching assistant will be expected to be an expert in all these areas (unless s/he happens to take a personal interest in the theatre and/or acting). What you certainly can do is to help groups to use the bullet points above when they are evaluating performances that they are taken to or see on screen. By this time, you should expect them to go much further than the Key Stage 1 children when asked to discuss a performance. Words such as 'characterisation' might be used or the children should be able to tell you in their own words about the importance of how the actors have portrayed their roles and what exactly they noticed as they watched them. They might have been fascinated by the use of lighting, scenery or sound effects, or they might feel the pace of the performance was a bit slow.

Drama and language knowledge

I mentioned above that drama offers interesting ways in to discussing the variety of spoken language on which native speakers can draw. For example, the teacher might decide to show the class a short recorded extract from a soap opera, perhaps where a child has done something naughty like stealing from a shop and this is being discussed by the other characters. As a whole class, the children could identify features of the language used – it's likely to be colloquial (chatty) and informal English. Perhaps you might hear words and expression such as:

- Nicking something;
- I never done nothing;
- He's always been a load of trouble to his mum, that lad.

You might be asked to help a group of children to recast this episode into another form, or genre as it is sometimes called. One possibility would be a policewoman presenting her report in court. As already mentioned (in Chapter 1) adults have more experience of life and of a range of social situations than children – they usually have a clearer view of what would/would not be said on a particular occasion. These are some of the issues you might help the children to identify:

- 'Nicking' is a slang word. The policewoman would refer to 'stealing' unless she was directly quoting what someone else had said. It's not that 'nicking' is wrong but it's not appropriate for this situation.

- 'I never done nothing' is an example of a double negative because both 'never' and 'nothing' are negative expressions. This way of expressing the negative is frequently used in some parts of Britain, and indeed two words are always used in some other languages (in French for example, both 'ne' and 'pas' are used). In standard English, it's customary only to use one negative word: 'I didn't do anything'.

- 'A load of trouble' is another colloquial expression that an officer would be unlikely to use when giving evidence in court (though of course she might well use it off-duty).

- The structure of the last sentence is typical of informal speech, with 'that lad' tagged on at the end. You could ask the children to think about how the sentence could be reshaped to make it sound more formal (e.g. 'That boy/lad has always been a lot of trouble to his mother').

Before leaving this topic, I must emphasise again that the point of doing this kind of work is not to suggest the sloppy way in which some of us speak – rather we are helping the children to think about the rich variety of vocabulary and syntactical choices that English offers us, and the consequences of choosing one form rather than another on a specific occasion. I sometimes find it quite difficult to discuss these consequences: it can raise difficult issues about the fact that England is still a very class-ridden society, issues which are not easy for young children to understand. 'It's that wretched class thing that always comes and whacks you in the face', as Michael Morpurgo commented (*Sunday Times* 18/4/04). Our choice of words categorises us in ways similar to those that children will use to categorise each other, i.e. according to the kind of mobile phone they own or the make of jeans they wear. An explicit discussion of these issues may be more appropriate at a later stage of schooling. The implicit knowledge of the range of ways in which people speak is apparent from a very early age, as you will realise if you listen to children enjoying role play in the home corner or the playground.

Geography/mathematics/PSHE/citizenship/English/drama

The next example offers the teacher an opportunity to combine speaking and writing in each of the above subject areas, but for the purposes of this book I will concentrate largely on the spoken elements. I have chosen to describe this particular topic because it illustrates a range of ways of speaking and listening, and because many of them are quite challenging for Key Stage 2 children, incorporating some of those more formal elements of spoken language described above.

An environmental survey

This is a real situation for a particular school in a particular village but I am not aware of whether or not they have carried out work like this! The village is strung out along a busy main road, with a primary school and a high school some hundred yards distant from each other on the same side of the road, and a church almost opposite the primary school. Both schools start at the same time, and as the schools are in a rural area, a large number of buses bring the children to the high school. Most children these days are taken to the primary school in their parents' cars. There is a primary school car park, though it's a short walk from the school. There is no high school car park.

The children's task would be to survey the situation, gather facts and figures and a range of opinions and work towards a 'public meeting' where children, in role, could put forward the views of all the interested parties. Written outcomes could include letters – perhaps to the local newspaper – posters and a report of the views expressed at the meeting.

Opportunities for talking and learning

I am assuming, as always throughout this book, that your role would be to help the teacher to explore this situation, not to set it up yourself. As with drama, the presence of another adult can be enormously supportive.

Geography for Key Stage 2 in the National Curriculum suggests many appropriate learning objectives. Children are expected to be able to:

- collect and record evidence (perhaps by producing a graph);
- analyse evidence and draw conclusions;
- identify and explain different views that people, including themselves, hold about geographical issues;
- communicate in ways appropriate to the task and audience;
- use appropriate geographical vocabulary.

In the early stages of the project, you might find yourself supporting a group of children in their planning talk. You might be encouraging them to find and use sources of secondary information such as aerial photographs, statistics and other information texts. They will need to prepare sketch maps of the locality and they may be required to use ICT skills to create a data file.

If the children are working in groups, they will probably need to allocate jobs – some tasks may be more popular than others. Gathering information through interviews and questionnaires is an interesting area but quite difficult techniques need to be employed if the children are to get 'rich pictures' from the people they talk to. They may also need help to under-stand that sometimes people will have strong vested interests which can cause them to take a biased view of the situation. Should one school start earlier in the morning than the other one, for example? But then some teachers, who may have long journeys already, will have to make an even earlier start. Why should they want to do that?

Once the data has been collected, children will need to discuss and analyse it. Decision-making skills will be important – there may be a range of possi-ble solutions favoured by different groups. One interesting technique is for each group to send an emissary to another group to find out what they are thinking and report back. The groups may then amend their own ideas in the light of the new ideas. Alternatively, the project could be set up in a different way with each child starting off in a 'home group' but then spend-ing some time in an 'expert group'. Each expert group would take on a different task: some might count the number of vehicles each morning for a week; some might measure the distance from the primary school to its (presently underused) car park; some might carry out interviewing tasks or analyse questionnaires. One member of each expert group would then return to the home groups and share the information obtained from the expert group. This is a good way of working because it gives each child a genuinely significant task to carry out – they are not telling their peers something they know already. It is important in this situation that the teaching assistant ensures that all the home groups do receive all the information necessary to go on to the next stage of the work. I will not dwell here on the various kinds of writing that might be done, though many of these would be collaborative and would necessitate some planning and decision-making.

A major outcome for the project would be a 'village meeting'. Roles would need to be allocated – perhaps by the teacher and you on this occa-sion, as some of them are likely to be quite challenging. A good chairperson, for example, would be crucial. Children at this age may need some help if they agree to put forward a view that they themselves are not actually in sympathy with. Enforcing the use of the car park, for example, would not be popular with those children who hate walking – especially on wet mornings! Yet someone should be found to speak up for this option at the meeting – perhaps 'the vicar' who is fed up with having the entrance to the church blocked by parked cars. But being 'the vicar', she will put her case calmly and diplomatically. Other participants might be expected to get a little more heated, perhaps attacking the 'representative of the parish council' for being so slow to take action. Then what? Someone should try to calm things down and bring the meeting back to order. What will 'the meeting' decide to do as a way forward?

If you were helping with the evaluation of this activity, many of the points I suggested on pages 86–7 would be useful to you here. In addition, you would be assessing the way the children have gathered, recorded and applied the factual data. You might comment on the use they made of geographical vocabulary and concepts. You might talk about their social skills in interviewing members of the various interest groups in the village, or their willingness to take on and support a range of ideas at the meeting.

In this chapter I can only give you a flavour of how oracy can support learning across the curriculum. I hope that the examples will help you to understand how throughout Key Stage 2, children can acquire the confidence – provided they have enough support – to tackle more and more demanding tasks under the four key headings suggested by the DfES/QCA material:

- Speaking
- Listening
- Group discussion
- Drama

To sum up the range of learning experiences that this work might encompass across all key stages, I still find it useful to refer back to a list drawn up by the Cumbria Oracy Project team (as long ago as 1988) because it's expressed in terms that make sense to practising teachers (and teaching assistants!):

- Talking and listening as somebody else.
- Talking and listening to investigate and/or find an answer.
- Talking and listening during a practical activity.
- Talking and listening to create and make something together.
- Talking and listening to find out what you know, think and feel.
- Talking and listening to tell or explain.

Summary

In this chapter I have looked at:

● Encouraging the reluctant talker at Key Stage 2.

● Working towards more formal speaking and listening outcomes.

● Validating talk as a significant way of learning.

● Helping children to reflect on their achievements as speakers and listeners.

● Developing talk through work in

 – drama

 – history

 – geography

 – PSHE/citizenship

 – English

 – mathematics

Further reading

DfES/QCA (2003a) *Speaking, Listening and Learning: Working with Children in Key Stages 1 and 2. Handbook.* London: DfES/QCA.

DfES/QCA (2003b) *Speaking, Listening and Learning: Working with Children in Key Stages 1 and 2. Teaching Objectives and Classroom Activities.* London: DfES/QCA.

Medwell, J., Moore, G., Wray, D. and Griffiths, V. (2002) *Primary English: Knowledge and Understanding.* Exeter: Learning Matters.

Wray, D. and Medwell, J. (2001) *Teaching English in Primary Schools* (2nd edn). London: Letts.

Wyse, D., Jones, R., Bainbridge, R. and Sarland, C. (2000) *Teaching English, Language and Literacy.* London: Routledge Falmer.

Chapter 7

The assessment of speaking and listening

In my experience, the assessment of speaking and listening is frequently a neglected area in primary schools. While some schools undoubtedly have systems in place, you should not be too surprised if your school does not. Part of the reason for this may be that there has been no SAT or national test equivalent to those for reading and writing. And, it must also be admitted, speaking and listening is not a straightforward aspect of language development to assess. I will outline some of the reasons why this is the case in more detail in this chapter, but one difficulty must be immediately obvious. Unlike a pile of exercise books or a collection of storybooks the children have made, examples of their speaking and listening cannot be taken home to be assessed. Speaking and listening must be assessed *in situ*. Recordings can be made, but they can be intrusive – especially video recordings. They can have an effect to some extent on the spontaneity of the discussion; the microphone has to be in the right place at the right time to capture what is said. Much of the richness of the situation is lost if only the words are being heard and tapes are time-consuming to listen to. Nevertheless, there may be times when it's worthwhile making a recording and I will look at some of these, but on the whole, other means of assessment must usually be sought.

Why assess speaking and listening?

Assessment is only worthwhile if it provides information that can help:

● to improve a child's individual performance, formatively, on a week-by-week or term-by-term basis;

- to hand on informative records at the end of a year or a key stage;
- to enable teachers to gauge whether their methods and approaches have been successful;
- to cast light on how the children are performing in comparison with other schools in similar catchment areas and with schools nationally.

Considerations which should inform the assessment process

There are always social dimensions to any form of assessment: it never takes place in a social or cultural vacuum. In the case of speaking and listening, it's particularly important to be aware of them. Here are just a few.

- Some children are confident speakers – it's part of their nature to take the lead in a discussion. Some are naturally quiet types. Some will talk freely in some contexts – perhaps at home (or at school) – but they will be silent in other situations. Talk is very context-dependent. Before children are commented on or given a grade as speakers and listeners, they need to be heard in a number of contexts.

- Some schools may traditionally have had a preferred model of pupil behaviour, a view of the 'ideal pupil' who is quiet, doesn't argue and only speaks when spoken to. Such schools must be aware that times have changed and the publication of the DfES/QCA materials (2003) on speaking and listening may have given some urgency to moves towards reform. But attitudes do not change overnight, particularly if some members of staff find it hard to adapt to different teaching approaches. And the assessment of oracy, more than anything else, must be a whole-school issue (see pp. 35–6).

- Schools may have different perceptions of what is appropriate behaviour for boys as distinct from that of girls. Girls may also acquire their own views – from home and from their peer group – about the image they want to project. I am not just thinking about what is traditionally expected from Muslim girls here – there are girls from all backgrounds who feel, for example, that it's not 'feminine' to have strong views and to defend them in class.

- There may be social class prejudices that interfere with an objective assessment by the teacher of a child's speaking and listening. Research suggests that children with more 'middle-class' speech habits are likely to be graded more highly than those with, say, a strong regional accent – even though the content of the talk may be almost identical. Looking at the person you are talking to, sitting up straight in the chair rather than slouching, avoiding overuse of mannerisms such as 'you know' or 'innit' – all these can sway the assessor towards a more favourable impression, perhaps subconsciously.

- Classrooms are places where people meet each other every day and spend a considerable amount of time together. This means that identities are built up and established over time, which can then be quite difficult to shake off. Someone who has become known as 'the class clown', for example, may find it hard to get a thoughtful hearing, even when they are not trying to make people laugh. It's not like saying something to a person one meets in a train and never sees again – your words can come back to haunt you. If you make a slip and say something that others find funny, they may never let you forget it. It's best to be cautious. In my own research into speaking and listening in a Year 6 class, I found that there were hierarchies of power and influence among the pupils. If you found yourself in X's group, it was not a good idea to argue with what he wanted to do – silent acquiescence was far more sensible.

What is being assessed?

It's important for you and the teacher to be clear – and to make sure the children are clear – about whether the talk itself is being assessed or the learning that has been achieved through talk. Sometimes it seems difficult to separate them because obviously the children are always talking about *something*. We wouldn't want children in school making conversation just for the sake of it. As far as schools and classrooms are concerned, the talk will usually be linked to a National Curriculum learning objective.

In any talk situation there always three elements:

- COMMUNICATIVE
- SOCIAL
- COGNITIVE

What this means is that the teacher may be primarily concerned with **communicative** aspects – judging how well the children have put their ideas across and how effectively they have drawn on the talk and listening skills discussed in earlier chapters. Alternatively s/he may want to assess how well the children have worked together as a group (the **social** aspects). If the teacher wants the assessment to focus on the **cognitive** skills, this means that what the children have learned by talking together is of paramount importance – in maths, science or any other curriculum area.

The assessment may, of course, have more than one focus, but trying to do too much at once makes life difficult for the assessor. Talk is very ephemeral – gone in the space of a few minutes, sometimes seconds. I have more to say about this on p. 106.

Agreeing on criteria

How will you know, when you are listening to children talking, that what you judge as successful – or excellent even – would be equally highly rated by the teacher? How did you reach your opinion in the first place? These questions raise the difficult issue of shared criteria. It is probably not possible or even desirable to break every talk situation down into individual elements in order to judge each one separately. When we assess, we usually take an overall view of communicative effectiveness. More will be expected of you, however, than just your impression. You should feel confident that at the back of your mind you have a checklist of significant elements that will help you to form your judgement. It will be important for you to have shared ideas on these significant elements, certainly with your teacher but preferably as a whole-school staff. Better still, the children too should be aware of the pegs on which will be hung the judgements of their speaking and listening. Let's consider each of the three aspects outlined above.

Cognitive aspects (learning *through* talk)

In some ways these are the most straightforward to assess. If you are focusing on these you are asking yourself: 'Has the group discussion, or the role play or whatever, resulted in the children learning x, y or z [the learning objectives]?' (x, y and z having been agreed on by you and the teacher beforehand). These objectives may have originated from the National Curriculum or the literacy or numeracy strategy documents. When the talking is over, the children will give a report back or answer some questions – perhaps do some written work even – which will give you a fairly clear idea about their understanding of the topics covered. If they have achieved those learning objectives, then to that extent their talk was good talk! If they have not/only partially learned them, steps can be taken to remedy the situation by some reading, some teacher input or even some further discussion.

Communicative and social aspects

If on a specific occasion these aspects are what you are mainly assessing, you will be looking not so much at what was learned in history, maths or whatever, but at how well the children have 'learned to talk' or to work together as an effective group. You might even decide to assess them on what they have learned 'about' talk as a consequence of the activity in which they were engaged.

This is fairly uncharted territory, particularly when it comes to judging the progress children are making week by week. Changes in their behaviour as speakers and listeners may be quite subtle and difficult to pin down. In the past, teachers have not had to provide evidence of progression to the same extent as they have for reading and writing. Admittedly, they have had the National Curriculum attainment targets to help them, but these are quite brief general descriptions lacking in specific detail and may not have been referred to very frequently. With the publication of the DfES/QCA materials on speaking and listening (2003), clear guidance has been given on sets of objectives on a term basis, but assessment of results is not discussed to the same extent (although there is a helpful video).

I hope that the information contained in this book has helped to give you the confidence to identify some of the crucial elements if you find yourself assessing some speaking and listening. A particular example might be useful. In a Key Stage 2 class, you might say to a group of children:

> This morning I shall be looking at how well you tackle [the task] in your group. You need to spend some time planning your strategy and then get started. I shall expect you to stop for a recap and a review of what you've done so far, just before break. I'll remind you when you've got 15 minutes left!

As you assess what the children do, you might be thinking about *some* of the following elements. There are too many to keep in mind all at once and you will probably have agreed with the teacher what your priorities are, given the particular circumstances. By the end of the session you should have some evidence concerning:

- ability to lead the group into getting the work underway;
- ability to bring everyone on board if some children are not focused;
- listening to others and showing a willingness to adapt to their ideas;
- knowing when to give in and when to press a minority view;
- explaining/clarifying something;
- asking useful questions;
- realising when planning needs to move on to action and getting everyone started;
- recapping skills;
- reconciling disagreements;
- reviewing what's been achieved, giving credit where it's due and summarising what the group still needs to do.

It's unlikely that every child will be assessed on this occasion (see p. 106).

I would like to emphasise that the above list (and that on p. 109) is there to inform your thinking, rather than being a checklist of things you must write about. The assessment process cannot be reduced to a compulsory tick list of items even though, as you may have noticed, there is a tendency to treat all aspects of education like this nowadays. I would like to see lists like these shared at a staff meeting and then gradually become part of people's thinking – to be used flexibly and according to circumstances, rather than to become set in stone.

Statementing and the assessment of speaking and listening

There may be occasions – perhaps when a particular child is causing concern and is being considered for a statement of special educational needs – when you and the teacher do want to draw up a very specific list of elements about which it would be useful to have detailed comments. You may be especially concerned, for example, about the child's ability to listen to and co-operate with others. In this situation, too, it is important to observe the child in a range of contexts – and at various times of the day and week. And it goes without saying that you would want to share this information with others, including carers and other teachers/teaching assistants.

Agreeing on standards

It's one thing for a school to discuss a shared list of elements to inform everyone's thinking about speaking and listening, it's another to agree on the standards children have achieved. Training videos and exemplification material do help, but perhaps the most useful process, albeit a time-consuming one, is sharing observations and notes with colleagues – even if you can only manage to do this very occasionally. In interpreting the National Curriculum attainment targets and agreeing on how the school will record the levels the children have achieved, there's an important role for the management team of the school, post-holders and special educational needs co-ordinators (SENCOs). You certainly should never feel that you are tackling any assessment unsupported.

Should you be assessing the children's ability to use standard English?

The short answer to this is 'Yes'. The National Curriculum Attainment Target for Speaking and Listening states that in order to achieve Level 3, children must 'begin to be aware of standard English and when it is used'. To progress to Level 4, they must 'use appropriately some of the features of standard English vocabulary and grammar'.

The DfES/QCA (2003) materials on speaking and listening endorse this view (as quoted on p. 82). However, there is some confusion. While emphasising the point which I also made earlier that it's very important to be clear about what is being assessed, the *Handbook* (DfES/QCA 2003a) actually appears to contradict itself. First, on page 30, we read that 'It's not children's accent or dialect that is being assessed', but a few lines further on we are told that they are to be assessed on 'clarity in communicating, including the use of reason, clear sequence of ideas *and standard English*' (emphasis added). Schools will have to be sensitive to local conditions and circumstances and decide when it is/is not appropriate to include the use of standard English as an assessment criterion.

Speakers of other languages

It's important that whenever possible the assessment of speaking and listening should include comments on a child's fluency in a community language. Sometimes it's difficult to assess the contribution a child is making, but at the very least, attention should be paid to the times when a child meets a new challenge in English. Co-operation with parents and those in the community who share the child's languages will also help to provide a fuller picture.

Assessing children's knowledge *about* language

This is an important strand, as I have been at pains to stress throughout this book, and should be recognised as such in a school's approach to the assessment of speaking and listening. In the Foundation Stage, for example, it would be interesting to note when a child whose first language is English begins to show an interest in the other languages spoken in the class. It might also be noted when children begin to use and appreciate standard English – or the accents and dialects of the other children, visitors or actors etc.

When can assessments be made?

In order to ensure fairness to a child, assessments should be made on a number of occasions so that s/he is recorded talking at different times of the day and the week, in different settings, for a range of purposes and with a variety of audiences.

During lesson times

The literacy hour and other English and drama sessions will offer plenty of opportunities, but, as you will have seen while you have been working in school, there is no subject in the National Curriculum which does not require children to participate in speaking and listening. It is when teachers are working in curriculum areas which are not specifically 'language-related' that they will probably have primarily cognitive aims (see above), but having a teaching assistant to support the assessment process makes it much easier to note the children's achievements in speaking and listening while the teacher concentrates on the teaching of the subject area.

More formal occasions

Much of the talking in lesson times will be informal and spontaneous. Opportunities should also be created, however, for children to be assessed in more formal situations, perhaps during an assembly, a 'sharing' session or when they are talking to a group that is larger than they are used to. I have in mind some occasion when they have had time to plan and even perhaps rehearse what they will say.

Outside the classroom

Chatting to parents can often shed more light on the child as a talker. Talk, as I have said, is very context-dependent and a surprising picture can emerge of a child who is quite different at school from at home – more silent *or* more talkative. This knowledge can alert the school to possible aspects of the child's circumstances which might need support. It's important to share with parents the achievements in speaking and listening that the school has observed. Most parents are now seeing development in these areas as a central part of school life, on a par with reading and writing. It's vital to enlist their understanding and help.

Set piece occasions

All the above require assessment of speaking and listening to be done 'on the hoof' but of course it is possible to set up assessment situations. Traditionally, children have been asked to prepare a talk on a hobby, for example, which would shed light on their capacity to cope with the kind of planned and rehearsed talk already referred to. But there are many other possibilities. In my area, children have the opportunity to take part annually in a Book Event where teams of four children are questioned on a book they have all read. They know the kinds of questions they may be asked, but must work together as a group to answer the questions on the day. This is an interschool competitive event and is held in front of an audience, but there is no reason why something like this should not be set up in the classroom. It is quite time-consuming but the help of a teaching assistant would make it possible to carry out.

Children could also be given a range of 'talk tasks' to carry out over a given period, deciding for themselves when they are ready to do them. These could include:

- Reading something out loud in assembly.
- Making a telephone call for the teacher.
- Meeting a visitor to the school.
- Interviewing someone unknown to them for the school newspaper.
- Giving a talk to the class using visual aids, the whiteboard or the OHP.

How can assessments be made?

Given that I seem to have asked rather a lot of you in this chapter so far, you are probably keen to hear how you can manage it all!

Children self-assessing: reflecting with each other on how they are progressing

For this to be successful, we need to share with children the kinds of thinking about speaking and listening discussed in this chapter. Many children, even in Year 1 and Year 2, have surprisingly good group skills. They should be given a lot of praise and encouragement when these are observed. As they progress through Key Stage 2 and become more reflective about the processes of learning, notes about the speaking and listening and group skills could form the basis of posters for the classroom walls. An example might look like this:

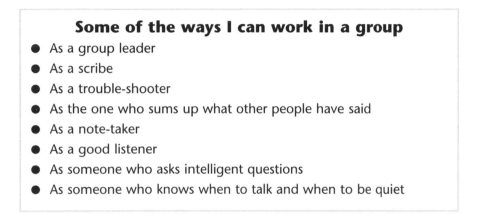

Some of the ways I can work in a group

- As a group leader
- As a scribe
- As a trouble-shooter
- As the one who sums up what other people have said
- As a note-taker
- As a good listener
- As someone who asks intelligent questions
- As someone who knows when to talk and when to be quiet

The poster could be added to and made more complex as the children progress through Key Stage 2. Teachers are familiar with helping children to become better readers and writers – they give them models and offer lots of advice and feedback. This should be extended to spoken language.

Talk diaries or talk logs

In Key Stage 2, this would be part of the self-assessment process. Children would be asked to make entries, perhaps at specified times, similar to their reading record (see *Supporting Reading* in this series). They could 'tell the story' very briefly of what they have done. They could just choose from a list the kinds of talk they have been involved in: persuading, storytelling, describing etc., but I think the diary is more useful if they say a little bit more than that, e.g.:

> I discussed with Gary how we were going to . . .
>
> I told a story to the whole class without using any notes . . .
>
> I read out my piece about X in assembly and explained how . . .

I listened to a video about…and made notes…

I explained to five other people how to…

Each entry should be dated and record the purpose of the talk, in a context, with a note of who or how many people took part. It might be important to comment on the setting:

I gave a report in the village hall on the results of our traffic survey.

I asked people questions outside the village shop.

I interviewed the lady at the library.

The children should be encouraged to comment on any features they were especially pleased with or felt concerned about:

Everybody said I used my visual aids really well.

The group was very big and I felt scared.

There should also be space for the teacher and other adults to add comments.

Simplified talk diaries could also be kept in Key Stage 1, but they would be completed by the teacher or teaching assistant with the child's help. A pro-forma like that on p. 107 could be used. If time is short, items could be merely ticked with no additional comments. The pro-forma could be amended for each year group to include EAL speakers and children with special needs. Keeping a talk log validates the importance of talk from the very beginning and helps children begin to see what's expected of them.

Teacher records

One of the difficulties about assessment is the time it takes. This is particularly true when, as is the case with speaking and listening, it must be fitted into the teaching day to a large extent. It will probably not be realistic, even with the help of a teaching assistant, to assess more than two or three children's oracy skills each week.

One way to keep such records is to have a page for each child in a loose-leaf file – or these days, more probably, on a disc. Quick jottings on paper can be made to be written up later, but in fact you will probably find that,

Talk diary for _____

Class_____

Week beginning _____

Purpose	Comments
I talked to the whole class.	
I listened to a story.	
I said 'please' and 'thank you'.	
I asked nicely for something I needed.	
I stopped talking when I was asked to.	
I played a game with . . .	
I took a message to . . .	
I answered my name when Mrs X was taking the register.	
The thing I am most pleased about is . . .	
Parent's comment:	

provided you make entries fairly regularly on your chosen two or three children, you will remember what you want to note down.

If you are working in the Foundation Stage, you might want to compile a more fully-fledged record with photographs or examples of things the child has made and written, together with contributions from the parents and the children. At this stage, most of the assessment the child undertakes is likely to be oral, so records of these assessments would also be included.

It might be useful, occasionally, to have a specific objective and to use it to monitor the whole class. In this instance, a class list could be used to record which children exceed or fall short of expectations. In the World War II project, for example (see p. 84), the objective could be 'sustaining and developing a role over a five-week period'.

The DfES/QCA materials (2003a) offer a record sheet which teachers can use, and examples are given of how it has been used. A copy of the record sheet is shown on p. 109.

So far in this section, ongoing weekly records have been discussed, but at the end of a year or a key stage, a 'statement of oral achievement' could be drawn up, negotiated with, and perhaps partly written by, the children. This could be taken home and later discussed with parents. It should also, of course, be shared with the children's next teacher and with those, such as teaching assistants, who will be working with them and trying to take them further.

Set piece assessments

On the whole, I believe that it is more useful to assess children as they go about the regular classroom activities, but sometimes it is useful to set up a specific assessment activity. If these are organised, 'it's possible to make more judgements about more children because the criteria are clear and the teacher knows what to listen for' (DfES/QCA 2003a: 29).

An example might be the teams of children discussing something they have read (mentioned on p. 104). It would be important to share with the children what you and the teacher will be listening for:

● Does everyone in the group get a chance to speak?

Speaking and listening		Record sheet
Name and year	**Activity/date**	**Assessment comments**
Speaking for different audiences: • clarity, intonation, pace • organisation, use of detail • adaptation to audience • use of standard English		
Listening and responding: • understands main points • asks relevant questions • responds appropriately		
Group interaction and discussion: • takes different roles • supports others, takes turns • makes contributions to sustain and complete the activity		
Drama and role play: • improvises and sustains role • plans, performs and evaluates plays • works with others in performance		
Next steps:		

● Do you listen to and respond to each other's ideas?

● Do you provide evidence that you have read the book carefully?

● Do you speak clearly and in a way that keeps the listeners' interest?

The results could form an additional sheet in the children's talk diary or log book to be shared with them and their parents.

Target setting

One of the main purposes of assessment is to inform future planning and it would be encouraging to see all these methods of assessment used to agree on specific targets for each child, in the same way as they are now for literacy and numeracy. These would be reviewed on a termly or half-termly basis.

Summary

In this chapter I have looked at:

● The reasons for assessing speaking and listening.

● Considerations which should inform the assessment process.

● What is being assessed.

● Agreeing on criteria.

● Agreeing on standards.

● When to assess.

● How to manage assessment.

Further reading

Boys, R. (2002) 'Communication, language and literacy', in I. Keating (ed.) *Teaching Foundation Stage*. Exeter: Learning Matters.

DfES/QCA (2003a) *Speaking, Listening and Learning: Working with Children in Key Stages 1 and 2. Handbook*. London: DfES/QCA.

DfES/QCA (2003b) *Speaking, Listening and Learning: Working with Children in Key Stages 1 and 2. Teaching Objectives and Classroom Activities*. London: DfES/QCA.

Index